D1739070

Continued Praise for
The Tears of Things

"Another shining gift from one of our greatest Christian teachers . . . Fr. Richard Rohr has been such an inspiration to so many of us."
—BRIAN D. MCLAREN, author of *Life After Doom*

"In these insightful and beautifully written reflections, Richard Rohr explores the teachings of the prophets, helping us discover how deeply God loves us in the midst of our hurtful and misguided ways."
—JAMES FINLEY, psychologist and author of *The Healing Path*

"Fr. Richard Rohr invites us into a relationship with sadness as the path to knowing how actively God works with us. If we stop being absorbed in our personal dramas, if we fearlessly open to the human condition, we discover the boundlessness of the human heart—compassion not only for people, but for how we continue to create our own suffering."
—MARGARET WHEATLEY, author of *Restoring Sanity*

"Richard Rohr offers a path forward beyond dying religions and moribund civilizations, one that marries mysticism and prophecy. Reminding us that evil flourishes best when it is denied, he credits the prophets for having started the move from religion to spirituality that is beckoning us today. Rohr has saved his best book for the last."
—MATTHEW FOX, Episcopal priest and author of *Original Blessing*

BY RICHARD ROHR

The Universal Christ
Everything Is Sacred

THE
TEARS
OF
THINGS

PROPHETIC WISDOM FOR
AN AGE OF OUTRAGE

RICHARD
ROHR

CONVERGENT
NEW YORK

Scripture quotations marked (JB) are from the Jerusalem Bible
© 1966 by Darton Longman & Todd Ltd. and Doubleday and Company Ltd.

Scripture quotations marked (NRSV) are taken from the New Revised Standard Version
Bible, copyright © 1989 National Council of the Churches of Christ in the
United States of America. Used by permission. All rights reserved worldwide.

Scripture quotations marked (KJV) are taken from the King James Version.

Published in the United States by Convergent Books,
an imprint of Random House, a division of
Penguin Random House LLC, New York.

CONVERGENT with colophon is a registered trademark of
Penguin Random House LLC.

Unless otherwise stated, Richard Rohr uses his own translation and/or
paraphrase of Scripture. Father Richard draws from a variety of English translations,
including the Jerusalem Bible (JB), New American Standard Bible (NASB),
New English Translation (NET), J.B. Phillips New Testament (Phillips),
Revised Standard Version (RSV), and The Message (MSG).

Grateful acknowledgment is made to Rosemerry Wahtola Trommer for permission
to reprint "For When People Ask" from *All the Honey* by Rosemerry Wahtola Trommer
(Samara Press, 2023), copyright © 2023 by Rosemerry Wahtola Trommer.
Reprinted by permission of the poet.

LIBRARY OF CONGRESS CATALOGING-IN-PUBLICATION DATA
Names: Rohr, Richard, author.
Title: The tears of things / by Richard Rohr.
Description: New York, NY: Convergent, [2025]
Identifiers: LCCN 2024035567 (print) | LCCN 2024035568 (ebook) |
ISBN 9780593735817 (hardback) | ISBN 9780593735824 (ebook)
Subjects: LCSH: Bible. Prophets—Criticism, interpretation, etc. |
Good and evil—Biblical teaching. | Violence—Biblical teaching. |
Spiritual life—Biblical teaching.
Classification: LCC BS1505.52 .R65 2025 (print) | LCC BS1505.52 (ebook) |
DDC 224/.06—dc23/eng/20240909
LC record available at https://lccn.loc.gov/2024035567
LC ebook record available at https://lccn.loc.gov/2024035568

Printed in the United States of America on acid-free paper

convergentbooks.com

2 4 6 8 9 7 5 3 1

First Edition

Book design by Elizabeth A. D. Eno

To Sheryl Fullerton, my long-suffering and brilliant editor,
who labored over my many incomplete, incorrect,
and poorly stated ideas to bring this book to print.

To Lee Staman, our worthy librarian and scholar at
the Center for Action and Contemplation, who
assured me that my major thesis here was true.

FOR WHEN PEOPLE ASK

I want a word that means
    okay and *not okay,*
        more than that: a word that means
devastated and *stunned with joy.*
    I want the word that says
        I feel it all all at once.
The heart is not like a songbird
    singing only one note at a time,
        more like a Tuvan throat singer
able to sing both a drone
    and simultaneously
        two or three harmonics high above it—
a sound, the Tuvans say,
    that gives the impression
        of wind swirling among rocks.
The heart understands swirl,
    how the churning of opposite feelings
        weaves through us like an insistent breeze
leads us wordlessly deeper into ourselves,
    blesses us with paradox
        so we might walk more openly
into this world so rife with devastation,
    this world so ripe with joy.

                —Rosemerry Wahtola Trommer[1]

A hand was there, stretching out to me and holding a scroll. . . . On it was written lamentations, weeping, and moanings. . . . I opened my mouth; he gave me the scroll to eat. . . . I ate it, and it tasted sweet as honey. (Ezekiel 2:9–10; 3:2–3)

CONTENTS

Good Trouble

When we picture a prophet of the Old Testament—and there are many of them, more than thirty, including seven women[1]—most of us imagine an angry, wild-haired person ranting and raving at the people of Israel for their many sins or predicting future doom. Some of the prophets did just that, but my years of study, conversation, and contemplation have shown me that this prevailing image is not the truest or most important reality of their work, calling, or messages.

It's true that the prophets called Israel, many times, to return to the covenant God made with them at Mount Sinai. After leading the people out of Egyptian slavery, God supplied the law, including the Ten Commandments, that was meant to govern and shape their lives in the Promised Land. They were to refrain from lying, stealing, committing adultery, and so on.

This was Morality 101, the basic order without which a society cannot maintain itself. But the people usually fell short, often disastrously so. They substituted purity codes and performance for the spirit of that law. They forgot not only what they had promised but also how much and how deeply Yahweh cared for them. There was a deep need, then and now, for someone who would call the people to return to God and to justice. Someone who would warn them, critique them, and reveal God's heart to them. We call them prophets, and every religion needs them.

For hundreds of pivotal years—starting around 1300 B.C. and continuing through the eras of Israel's kingdom, exile, and conquest—prophets like Samuel, Jonah, Amos, Isaiah, Jeremiah, and Ezekiel performed this utterly important task. Besides being truth-tellers, they were radical change agents, messengers of divine revelation, teachers of a moral alternative, and deconstructors of every prevailing order. Both Isaiah 58 and Ezekiel 3 describe a prophet as a "sentry" or a "watchman," whose job is to hold Israel maddeningly honest, and to stop the Israelites from relying on arms, money, lies, and power to keep themselves safe and in control.

In this way, they introduced a completely novel role into ancient religion: an officially licensed critic, a devil's advocate who names and exposes their own group's shadow side! Few cultures, if any, develop such a counterintuitive role. By nature, civilization is intent on success and building, and has little time for self-critique. We disparage the other team and work ceaselessly to prove loyalty to our own. Maybe that's why the prophets seem most active from the time after Moses until about five centuries before Jesus, when Israel returned from exile in Babylon. After the exile, except for the moralisms of Malachi and the scattered fragments of Zechariah 9–14, there seems to be a lack of interest in the prophets, and their voices largely disappear from the scriptural account. Maybe that is why the people of Jesus's time were not ready for him. Their religious and spiritual community was too dispersed to know how to maintain a strong inner spiritual life. External obser-vance had taken over, symbolized by the oft-repeated New Testament opponents of Jesus, the scribes and the Pharisees.

In the gospel of Matthew, Jesus minces no words in critiqu-ing this scenario:

> Woe to you, scribes and Pharisees, hypocrites! For you tithe mint, dill, and cumin, and have neglected the weightier matters of the law: justice and mercy and faith. It is these you ought to have practiced without neglect-ing the others. You blind guides! You strain out a gnat but swallow a camel. (Matthew 23:23–24, NRSV)

The same dynamics operate today, with those in power or trying to gain power more interested in protecting their own interests and positions than in seeking justice. If you are a Christian, you might have seen a few paintings or stained-glass windows of a prophet pointing to Jesus, and that might have been their only supposed function! I'm convinced that unless we know the lineage, the exact genre, and the unique approach of the Hebrew prophets, we really can't understand Jesus.

Without prophets, we have settled for violent revolutions and righteous reformations in just about every century. Societ-ies have had no mechanism for reforming from within, and so our histories became about ferreting out heretics, imprisoning and murdering would-be rebels, and protecting shifting, angry, dualistic, and ambitious in-groups, each of which was more invested in their own rightness than the previous group.

Revolutions took the place of evolutions, in which both order and disorder are allowed to work together.[2] This is not a good way to move forward.

If we look at what prophets do and how they do it, we can see that they follow a classic pattern. When prophets see that the status quo is not working, they encourage what I call "holy disorder," a scenario in which the fundamental conditions and relationships of the group are disrupted (as when the Israelites were conquered by the Babylonians or persecuted by their enemies). This disruption can take positive form or negative form. Either God outgrows our present, limited understanding and we grow with God (as I wrote in my book *Falling Upward*),[3] or we regress due to our inability to love and trust what is happening. Then society reverts to legalism and formality until it ultimately disintegrates. From these disruptions, a new order arises (what I call "reorder"), in which human relations can work at a higher level that is more imaginative, less dualistic, and usually less violent than the first order or the reactive disorder.

The process of allowing and creating holy disorder is surely what Representative John Lewis called getting into "good trouble." He was referring to the good and necessary trouble of civil disobedience in the pursuit of racial justice, but his philosophy is equally powerful when we think about the prophets. For them, good trouble and holy disorder could draw forth better things—an entirely different consciousness characterized by more justice, more mercy, greater closeness to God. Of course, the process is never linear, and it never stops. The new reorder soon becomes a new order, and we need prophets to keep us from idolizing the new status quo. The only thing more dangerous and more common than narcissism is group narcissism. We have always needed a mechanism for positive change that is organic and comes from within, although we did not usually know that.

This full cycle of reorder is hard to imagine because it seldom happens in history. For example, I find it interesting that we Catholics have the sacrament of "holy orders," which is given to everyone who becomes a priest, but no ritual for holy disorder, even though prophecy was listed as the second-most-important gift of the Holy Spirit—more important than teaching or even miracles (1 Corinthians 12:28, Ephesians 4:11). We must ask, *Why has critical thinking always had to come from outside our religious systems and hardly been allowed from within?* This is a major problem.

We have tried to reform religion with the same codes of violence and willpower used by corporations, monetary systems, landowners, and nation-states, often leaving the egos and self-interests of hierarchs quite in control. Further, we have a tendency to minimize evil, attacking it in individual "bad guys" instead of exposing and convicting the intergenerational lies that consume most cultures: things like pride, deceit, power, war, and greed.

This, more than any other reason, is why Christianity did little to reform or evolve the Roman, Holy Roman, Russian, French, Spanish, English, or American empires, but instead slept comfortably with every one of them. The evils that ate us alive were seldom called evil because the "priestly" groups were intent on enforcing ritual requirements and purity codes—in which Jesus and the prophets showed little or no interest. Once we lose the prophetic analysis, most evil will be denied, disguised, or hidden among the rules and rituals of *religion and the law itself.* This is how truth is "discerned" in a dualistic world: by winning the purity and identity contests.

The philosopher Ken Wilber famously wrote that our path

to maturity usually involves some form of "cleaning up," "growing up," "waking up," and "showing up," more or less in that order.[4] Too often, though, we settle for merely cleaning up our behavior. I can only think of Pope Francis's recent clarification about the basic meaning of blessings. They are given not to people who have jumped the hoops of supposed moral worthiness, but to people who ask for one! Waking up is often devastatingly simple. It all comes down to *overcoming your separateness and any need to protect it.*

We must be eternally conscious of this fact: *For the untransformed self, religion is the most dangerous temptation of all.* Our egos, when they are validated by religion, are given full permission to enslave, segregate, demean, defraud, and inflate— because all bases are covered with pre-ascribed virtue and a supposed hatred of evil. This is what the prophets expose in their wholesale assault on temple worship, priestly classes, self-serving commandments, and intergenerational wealth. "Be very careful here!" they keep shouting. The prophets know that religion is the best and that religion also risks being the worst. We love to choose sides and declare ourselves sinless and pure and orthodox ("right"), with little evidence that it is true. This is always a surprise to everyone except the prophets.

My favorite thing about the prophetic books of the Bible is that they show a whole series of people in evolution of their understanding of God. Like most of us, the prophets started not only with judgmentalism and anger but also with a superiority complex of placing themselves above others. Then, in various ways, that outlook falls apart over the course of their writings. They move from that anger and judgmentalism to a reordered awareness in which they become more like God: more patient like God, more forgiving like God, more loving like God.

Throughout Scripture, the prophets seem to emphasize one sin above all the rest: idolatry, our habit of making things "God" that are not absolute, infinite, or objectively good. They are ruthless, as well, toward the preoccupations of our private self, which always wants to put itself in the best light. The gospel of Luke points this out directly. After Jesus teaches a highly symbolic "lawyer" that to have eternal life, you are to "love the Lord your God with all your heart . . . and your neighbor as yourself," the lawyer asks piously, "And who is my neighbor?" The lawyer is asking not because he wants an honest answer, but because he is "anxious to justify himself" (Luke 10:27, 29, JB).

I would go so far as to say that any worship service that does not begin with a sincere and plaintive kyrie eleison had best be very careful. The plea for mercy at the beginning of many Christian worship services is a statement and a warning that we are moving onto holy ground. We most likely do not know what we are talking about when we speak of God, so we'd best start with humility. We all and forever need mercy. One wonders what our theologies and worship would look like if we always began with an honest statement of our *not* knowing the real nature of holy mystery.

Prophets, then, are full truth-tellers, not fortune-tellers. They pull back the veil to radically reframe our preferred storyline of history: the boring and predictable narrative of winners and losers, rewards and punishments. They are by definition those rare individuals who see reality in its fullness and dimension, rather than in dualities like totally right or totally wrong, all good or all bad.

There must be someone in every age who can tell the faith community, and society at large, *Your first egoic glance at life— and God—is largely wrong! And it is largely engendered by fear.*

"No one else is your problem," says the prophet. "You are your own problem. What you think is goodness is too often delusion, and what you think is bad just might be your spiritual best friend." In doing so, they offer not only criticism but also visions of a more just, more merciful, more peaceful society—and call the people to live into it. Any religion or philosophy that teaches group blindness instead of full seeing is standing in the way of such clarity.

As Isaiah put it, "Woe to those who call evil good and good evil, who substitute darkness for light and light for darkness, who substitute bitter for sweet and sweet for bitter" (Isaiah 5:20, JB). He is describing how all of us use words and feelings to deceive ourselves and others. For example, the American political party that most blatantly hates law and order is invariably the one that loudly repeats the words *law and order* at every convention. Meanwhile, the party that knows it should be for immigrants acts as though it does not really want them in their backyard. Leaders who rail against impurity are too often the ones with a mistress. When we lack self-knowledge, we will unconsciously project our disliked and unknown self onto others, condemning them for the very faults we share. It is no wonder, then, that most of the prophets were murdered, as Jesus notes accusingly in Matthew 23:31.

What a catastrophic arrangement! The French anthropologist and literary critic René Girard wrote that the Bible is unique in all world literature in spotting this universal human avoidance of our own dark side. Girard calls this projecting of our own faults and fears onto others "the scapegoat mechanism."[5] It is present in all cultures, but the Bible alone, he writes, sees clearly how scapegoating works. Girard insists that scapegoating is what John was referring to when he described "the [universal] sin of the world" (John 1:29). The undoing of this tendency would be the task of any would-be savior for humanity and our continually fragile history. Yet it largely remains hidden in plain sight. *The Christian religion has sought to achieve its own innocence rather than act in solidarity with suffering and sinners.* This is a major point, I believe.

Religion worldwide, it seems, remains committed to making something or somebody a sacrifice in every age so that the status quo can be maintained. In our time, it is immigrants at the border; in other times it was Black people in the American South or Indigenous people being driven from their lands. But Jesus, René Girard insists, undoes sacrifice "once and for all" (Hebrews 7:27, 10:10, JB) by his revelation of an infinitely loving God. Such a god is very difficult to instrumentalize or use as a threat. As Paul tells us, in what might be the most subtle and well-argued piece of theology in the New Testament, we are no longer held captive "to the old written code." After Jesus, we are discharged from the law and free in "the new life of the spirit" (Romans 7:6, NRSV). In short, the prophets and Paul teach that law is never to be an end in itself, but only a boundary for the inflated human ego and a protector of the common good. Paul devotes three whole chapters of Galatians (3–5) and most of Romans to making this point.

The prophet's job was always spotting where the problem really lies: in the accusing ones themselves and in the delusions of the collective. They point out the universal illusion: "Because your stone throwing is bad, my stone throwing is good." And if the problem is really located in every group's aimlessly followed cultural agreements, it cannot be dumped on a few scapegoats, leaving those of us who are "more righteous" innocent and free of guilt or shame.

For spotting the hidden, communal, and disguised nature of sin and evil, the Jewish prophets have no parallels. They are merciless about truth and the disguises that individuals and groups adopt to protect their egos. Prophets call out not only those in power for their corruption and neglect but also the whole system of temple worship and sacrifice. As Amos puts it, "They lie on ivory beds, and sprawl on their divans, they dine on lambs from the flock, and bawl to the sound of the harp, . . . but about the ruin of the house of Joseph they do not care at all" (Amos 6:4–6, JB).

We have spent the centuries and millennia since constructing the same kinds of self-serving power centers that Jesus and the prophets denounced, and most of us are resigned to this status quo. When news broke of the extent of sexual abuse perpetrated by Catholic priests, for example, very few were surprised to learn how many cardinals and bishops and priests had ignored or tried to cover it up. We are rightly horrified by the violent abuse of the clergy. And yet, we are just not educated in or aware of the ways of structural sin, collective evil, or intergenerational trauma, much less cultural shadows—and we miss the bigger picture. It is not all malicious. We are accustomed to blaming individual bad people—and telling them to go to confession to deal with their personal sins. Any social analysis is still called by some "mixing politics with religion." But that's exactly what the prophets do. They call out the collective, not just the individual, as a way of seeking the common good and assuring us that some common good might just be possible. It is a lesson we still find hard to learn.

LEARNING TO LOVE AS GOD LOVES

When the prophet Moses was away on Mount Sinai, the rebellious Israelites, afraid he would not return, insisted on having a god they could see. His brother, the high priest Aaron, complied. He took all their gold jewelry and cast a golden calf that then became the center of their worship. Unlike Moses, Aaron was following the people's wishes rather than God's.

When Moses returned and saw what had happened, he ground down the golden calf into powder, mixed it with water, and made the Israelites drink what in his eyes was a needed medicine (Exodus 32:20). What a shocking, and profound, act. The prophet invariably makes you "drink" the taste of your poison so that you will avoid it, similar to much addiction work today.

Every priest seems to need a prophet, like Moses, and a sister prophetess, like Miriam, who can constantly expose their golden calves. Priests in the Aaronic tradition were preoccupied with creating rituals and sacrificial worship services—that they alone could lead. They tended to give the people what they wanted, so long as it benefited themselves. Aaron without Moses is always a problem in the making.

As a prophet, Moses acts as an antidote to Aaron's priestly dominance. Aaron creates and maintains the religious container, while Moses makes the container worth preserving and enjoying. Similarly, in the scriptural account of the Exodus, Aaron and Moses's sister, the prophetess Miriam, leads the music, the dancing, and the songs of praise after the Israelites' escape from Egypt (Exodus 15:20–21).* I like to call it performative liberation. Moses, meanwhile, is the full liberation

---

* I must point out early that the Old Testament sadly includes no record of women prophets who wrote. In those pages, at least, they only act. Maybe that is part of their message. Miriam, Deborah, Huldah, and Anna are all prophetic protagonists who face difficulty personally rather than write about it. My guess is that today there are more women prophets than men, just because they've been excluded from various systems. I do hope someone explores the path of the prophet from a woman's perspective, because I'm incapable. I still hold my privilege and bias as a white, American, male clergyperson.

xxiv INTRODUCTION

theologian, forever seeking a balance between cult, code, and community as the Israelites wander through the wilderness. He is the first to fully model this new role that we now call "prophet." Moses brings the law down the mountain, and he also smashes it when he sees that the people have disobeyed and created the golden calf (Exodus 32:19). In these acts, he integrates order with disorder and thus merits his position as the likely founder of monotheistic religion and of prophecy strictly defined. Moses contains and encloses Aaron's tendency to heed the crowd rather than God (as he did with the golden calf) and thus makes Aaron effective and not fully idolatrous.

The prophets' acts of defeating ego and naming scapegoats are, I believe, why they are never going to be popular or much read, despite taking up such a large part of the Bible. Yet their message also demands that we "die before we die," and learn to see things through the eyes of an infinite love. Without such a love foundation, almost all religions and worldviews devolve into forms of sacrifice, in which we debase something (or someone) else in hopes of achieving worthiness. This is why Jesus talks about "dying to self," or why Buddhists emphasize "lens wiping" and "ego spotting," by which adherents remove whatever delusions and bad habits of mind are keeping them from seeing reality clearly. All transformative religions are, each in their own way, trying to defeat the imperial ego and reveal the always camouflaged shadow self. Yet we need to be bathed in the assurance of infinite love before we can risk such ego deflation. The prophets gradually move us toward and through such divine assurance.

You see, as the prophets knew so well, we like our illusions, we like having enemies, and we are quite accustomed to our wars and prejudices, as much as we insist the contrary. They make us feel morally superior, even heroic, like the archangel

Michael slaying the dragon and driving all evil out of heaven (Revelation 12:7–8, 20:2–3), thus dividing the whole of creation into absolute good and absolute evil, and leaving us, of course, on the side of absolute good. We see this up to our own time in the universal attraction to and the valorization of war, even when we are clearly acting in our own interests and what we are doing is not objectively good. Why does the commandment "Thou shalt not kill" suddenly not apply? Only Quakers, Amish, Mennonites, and recent teachers of nonviolence have had the courage to even ask this troubling question.

God is still in the very slow process of disenchanting us out of our love of winning and succeeding. The slow metamorphosis of our notions of God—from lion to lamb, from anger to tears, from lonely solitude to grateful community—is quietly taking place. Humanity *is* indeed growing up. The evidence is just hard to see unless we are exposed, at least once, to this prophetic kind of countercultural truth. Today, for example, I am in awe at the number of people who are sincerely and often totally value oriented without belonging to any organized group that would make them follow its rules. This is new, I think, at least on such a broad scale. You can have values without group belonging, although you will probably be less strategically effective without a team.

Basically, this is the number one lesson: We can learn to love others by closely observing how God loves us and all of creation. Often this will mean observing and imitating nature's universal song of praise, just as Saint Francis, Hildegard of Bingen, William Wordsworth, John Muir, and Mary Oliver all did. Just gazing for an extended period at a spring bulb pushing up from dark soil or a robin hopping across the lawn—or at anything in nature—will reveal God's utter gratuity and the sacredness of every created thing. That is how God sees. Most of us never learned the lessons to be found in this kind of contemplation of the mysterious movement of living and dying, because we started by reading human texts that portrayed God as angry, wrathful, judgmental, and punitive. We pretty much anthropomorphized all our gods, imagining they were as small and righteous as we are!

The prophets started out the same way, but they changed and grew up. That is a theme of themes in this small book. The Hebrew prophets would not allow Israel to be unfaithful to God's ever-faithful love, because they were confident in their covenant relationship (*hesed*) that had loved them into community and courage. It was God's consistent action toward them, not their own worthiness or status as the "chosen people," that made them "chosen"!

It reminds me of my little-boy self, who fully believed that I was the "chosen one," my mother's favorite out of the four of us kids. It was not objectively true, but the belief worked its magic on me. It was easy to believe I was God's chosen, just as I was "Dickie Boy" to both Mom and Dad. Chosenness draws us into both oneness and goodness, almost like a magnet. In the same way, the prophets brilliantly insist that the Israelites must focus on God as their source of identity and group solidarity. God made them both one and good at the same time—by contagion and by reflection.

In a Trinitarian worldview, *all reality is relationship at its core*.[6] This one single benevolent mirror presented itself to the Israelites and made them utterly safe, free, and true—and available for daily election and interaction, which we would rightly call prayer, especially group prayer and song. Yahweh was available to them as the God of Israel, and the prophets had to access this availability themselves by a mutual vulnerability, risk, and self-disclosure. Just as we do today.

Astoundingly, the prophets repeatedly described this relationship as a "marriage" with God. As Hosea puts it, "I will betroth you to myself for ever, betroth you with integrity and justice, with tenderness and love; I will betroth you to myself with faithfulness, and thus you will come to know Yahweh" (Hosea 2:19–20, JB). This intimacy is radical, totally unlike anything humanity had ever imagined of God! Or of itself. Even the word *know* is striking in the original Hebrew; it is the word usually used for intimate (or carnal) knowing. It seems we are wasting our time seeking rational dogmatic knowledge of Yahweh when this inner, intimate, secret knowing is what we have already been given—and what alone convicts us.

Yet the ancient Israelites, just like us, found the "salvation" of this marriage relationship impossible to live out and quite dangerous to trust. "I will save them by the Lord their God; I will not save them by bow or sword or battle, horse or horseman," Hosea outrageously promises (Hosea 1:7, KJV). In other words, their salvation will not be found in private purity, or in willpower, but in trustful union between Yahweh and Israel's collective. "I will heal their disloyalty, I will love them with all my heart," says Yahweh (Hosea 14:4, JB). To receive God's forgiveness and tender love is, in fact, to receive God's infinity in little doses, which might just be called days or hours. You cannot prove them or account for having experienced them; they just add up as you get older, if you are receptive. And even one dose, one tenth, or one hundredth of infinity is still infinity! Jesus called it a mere mustard seed—all that is needed, it seems (Mark 4:30–32).

Is this vision of the human-divine relationship as naïve as it sounds? Is it foolhardy to trust in a radical, ongoing arrangement of being chosen by Yahweh? I hope to demonstrate in this book that the prophets' answer is a complex no. In the prophets, religion—and indeed, humankind—appears to be slowly morphing from code, creed, and cult to a kind of *mutual presencing,* a gradually learned "nakedness and vulnerability" that requires deliberate and focused attention, receptivity, and persistent awareness on both sides. Like soft, quiet snow, our experience of God's love accumulates to a fullness. Like an expanding and deepening delta, it broadens into many undeniable rivulets. You know it. You see it. You don't "believe" in it.

The whole Bible can be seen as a chronicle of examples meant to assure us that we are not crazy if we accept this invitation to vulnerability before God and one another. Such an initial attitude of vulnerability, as my friend Brené Brown teaches so well, is where all relationships begin to blossom.[7]

I am calling this surprising letting down of defenses—from both sides—the prophetic "way of tears," as opposed to our more common ways of heroic willpower, commandment, obedience, force, anger, and legitimated violence. It takes an initial tender vulnerability ("wounding") to defeat our ego and to open us to full consciousness—which must include the scary unconscious! It is a movement, frankly, from the Ten Commandments to the eight beatitudes. A movement that the prophets illustrated for us twenty-five hundred years ago, and that we need—out of desire and desperation—to recover today.

My hope is that this small book might accelerate the pace of human and spiritual vulnerability by encouraging each of us to take a first daring step. My first task is surely to ask that you forgive me for struggling to formulate words and concepts of such majesty and impact. It is wise, and no surprise, that the Hebrews insisted on never pronouncing the name of Yahweh. This cosmic act of humility was fully intended to keep both religion and theology always searching. The linguist and historian Heinrich Zimmer said that "the best things cannot be talked about."[8] And yet, like composers in every language, we still try to write our endless love songs. We must attempt the same here.*

---

* For the sake of simplifying sentence structure, I will often resort to gender-specific pronouns for God. Along with forgiving the whole universe for being imperfect, most of us also have to forgive the severe limitations of the English language or any language. Surely this is why the Spirit gave believers the incoherent "gift of tongues"—to keep us from climbing another Tower of Babel of supposedly perfect words. We all know God is beyond gender.

THE
TEARS
OF
THINGS

CHAPTER 1

The Tears of Things

I n the first book of Virgil's *Aeneid* (line 462), the hero Aeneas gazes at a mural that depicts a battle of the Trojan War and the deaths of his friends and countrymen. He is so moved with sorrow at the tragedy of it all that he speaks of "the tears of things" (*lacrimae rerum*). As Seamus Heaney translates it, "There are tears at the heart of things"—at the heart of our human experience.[1] Only tears can move both Aeneas and us beyond our deserved and paralyzing anger at evil, death, and injustice without losing the deep legitimacy of that anger.

This phrase "the tears of things" has continued to be quoted and requoted in many contexts over the centuries. You can find it on war memorials, in the work of poets, in the music of Franz Liszt, and in Pope Francis's recent encyclical letter

"Fratelli Tutti." (I myself remember it because of a haggard, bent-over Latin teacher who would often enter the classroom moaning "*Lacrimae rerum*" several times before he began quizzing us. It might have been comic if it weren't so tragic!)

Because the phrase has no prepositions in Latin, it allows two meanings at the same time: Virgil seems to be saying that there are both "tears *in* things" and "tears *for* things." And each of these tears leads to the other. Though translators often feel compelled to choose one or the other meaning, I believe the poet implies it is both.

There is an inherent sadness and tragedy in almost all situations: in our relationships, our mistakes, our failures large and small, and even our victories. We must develop a very real empathy for this reality, knowing that we cannot fully fix things, entirely change them, or make them to our liking. This "way of tears," and the deep vulnerability that it expresses, is opposed to our normal ways of seeking control through willpower, commandment, force, retribution, and violence. Instead, we begin in a state of empathy *with* and *for* things and people and events, which just might be the opposite of judgmentalism. It is hard to be on the attack when you are weeping.

Prophets and mystics recognize what most of us do not— that *all things have tears and all things deserve tears.* They know that grief and sadness are doorways to understanding life in a non-egocentric way. Tears come from both awe and empathy, and they generate even deeper awe and deeper empathy in us. The sympathy that wells up when we weep can be life-changing, too, drawing us out of ourselves and into communion with those around us. This is continuously exemplified in the writings that we have received from the Hebrew prophets.

After a lifetime of counseling and retreat work—not to mention my own spiritual direction—I have become convinced that most anger comes, first of all, from a place of *deep sadness*. Years ago, when I led male initiation rites at Ghost Ranch, New Mexico, I would watch men's jaws drop open and their faces turn pale when I said this. Life disappoints and hurts all of us, and the majority of people, particularly men, do not know how to react—except as a child does, with anger and rage. It is a defensive, reactionary, and totally understandable posture, but it often goes nowhere, and only creates cycles of bitterness and retaliation.

Over time, the Hebrew prophets came to see this profound connection between sadness and anger. It was what converted them to a level of truth-telling that is deeply and forever true—which is the real sign of a prophet. They first needed to get angry at injustices, oppression, and war. Anger can be deserved and even virtuous, particularly when it motivates us to begin seeking a necessary change. But only until sunset, Paul says (Ephesians 4:26). If we stay with our rage and resentment too long, we will righteously and unthinkingly pass on the hurt in ever new directions, and we injure our own souls in ways we don't even recognize. This is killing our postmodern world.

In this way, the realization that all things have tears, and most things deserve tears, might even be defined as a form of salvation: *from ourselves and from our illusions.* The prophets knew and taught and modeled that anger must first be recognized, allowed—even loved!—as an expression of the deep, normally inaccessible sadness that all of us carry. Even Jesus, our enlightened one, "sobbed" over the whole city of Jerusalem (Luke 19:41) and at the death of his friend Lazarus (John 11:35). In his final "sadness . . . and great distress" in the Garden of Gethsemane (Matthew 26:37, JB), "his sweat fell to the ground like great drops of blood" (Luke 22:44, JB).

Anybody who's on the edge, disadvantaged in some way, or barred from a position of hegemony or power will naturally understand the tears of the prophets, with their gut-level knowledge of systemic evil, cultural sin, and group illusion. Black Americans might have seen white people act nice or speak of human equality, for example, but they knew we lived behind a collective lie. Collective greed is killing America today. We make everything about money—everything—and injustices like these will naturally leave us exasperated and ultimately sad. How can we look at the suffering taking place in Gaza, or the violence of Hamas, or the people dying in Ukraine and be anything but sad? It's sad beyond words or concepts. Only the body can know it.

I recently turned eighty. The older I get, the more it feels like I must forgive almost everything for not being perfect, or as I first wanted or needed it to be. This is true of Christianity, the United States, politics in general, and most of all myself. Remember, if you do not transform your pain and egoic anger, you will always transmit it in another form. This transformation is the supreme work of all true spirituality and spiritual communities. Those communities offer us a place where our sadness and rage can be refined into human sympathy and active compassion.

Forgiveness of reality—including tragic reality—is the heart of the matter. All things cry for forgiveness in their imperfection, their incompleteness, their woundedness, their constant movement toward death. Mere rage or resentment will not change any of these realities. Tears often will, though: first by changing the one who weeps, and then by moving any who draw near to the weeping. Somehow, the prophets knew, the soul must weep to be a soul at all.

READING THE PROPHETIC JOURNEY

I fully admit that the prophets are very hard to read. Their writings invariably start with long stretches of strident anger and judgment, leading many of us to close the book or focus on a few favorable one-liners. These authors sound too much like the clergy and the early authority figures who berated us or moved us away from deserved sadness with their moralistic, unhelpful warnings, like "Don't be sad" and "Everything happens for a reason." Yet there is more going on beneath the surface, even in the portions of these books that strike us as harsh or off-putting.

During the writing of this book, I had an enlightening visit from the author and teacher Meg Wheatley. Meg has done much excellent work in systems thinking, leadership, and organization, and in her later years she has rather calmly come to accept her vocation as a prophet.

She believes, together with the Choctaw elder and Episcopal bishop Steven Charleston, that prophets "appear first as an early warning system within any culture at risk."[2] They are trying to warn us against the suffering that *our own collective behavior is bringing upon us.* Unfortunately, most people today (and many of the biblical texts as well) attribute this suffering to direct retribution from God. This misdirects the healing message.

This has kept us at the magical level of thinking, instead of moving us toward the critical level of thinking that truly transforms culture and individuals. We cannot know God, cannot know love or trust, when our brains are hijacked by the three F's of *fight, flight,* and *freeze.* Many people appear to be living their whole lives in one or more of those states today. We now call it trauma or PTSD, and see it everywhere and recognize that it passes intergenerationally. I suspect that this is what the church was recognizing with its poorly named idea of "original sin."

To address this issue correctly is of urgent importance for biblical studies, for religion in general, and for all of us personally and spiritually. A transactional, magical understanding of original sin has often led people to belligerent anger, self-serving zeal, rash judgments about those who were not "correctly" baptized, and undeserved pontification about those who were. Without some kind of human and psyche-based understanding of sin, I only see this problem continuing in ever-new formulations for the rest of human history.

In the Sermon on the Mount, Jesus did not intend his statement "Blessed are those who weep" (Luke 6:1) to be sentimentalized or remain unnoticed. Hard-heartedness, or what Zechariah and other prophets called "hearts of flint," prevented the people from hearing the law and the words that Yahweh had sent by the Spirit. A heart of stone cannot recognize the empires it builds and the empires it worships. Lamentation does. It moves us through anger and sadness, empowering us to truly hear and respond to the always-tragic now.

The prophet Ezekiel says it like this: "I shall give you a new heart, and put a new spirit in you; I shall remove the heart of stone from your bodies and give you a heart of flesh instead. I shall put my spirit in you. . . . You shall be my people and I will be your God" (Ezekiel 36:26–28, JB). This is the apotheosis of all healthy religion, the organ transplant that we all long for, the interior religiosity that all spirituality seeks.

Of course, language about God having emotions is always a projection of our human emotions onto God. But if we can understand that God weeps over the human situation—as Jesus wept over the city of Jerusalem, again over Lazarus's death, and in Gethsemane—we know it's a universal truth. Instead of being hateful, God is sad and pitying. The English Dominican theologian Gerald Vann wrote a book called *The Divine Pity* and made much the same point. God doesn't hate anything God created, but God pities it in the true meaning of the word *pity*, which is to have compassion for the suffering of everything.

By following the prophets' *full journey* from anger to sadness and beyond, we can mature in belief, as they had to do themselves. All the prophets started with anger, or even rage, at all the right things: injustice, oppression, deceit, misuse of money, power, even religion itself. But with only a couple of exceptions (Nahum and Obadiah, who remained angry), they did not stop there. They were not just reformers; they were also mystics who were captivated by the wholeness and beauty at the heart of reality at the same time as they were confronting injustice. I hope to make those distinctions clear in this book. We miss the point when we confuse prophets with mere liberal humanists.

Truth and prophecy must be subjected to the refiner's fire of discernment. As we are slowly discovering with wildfires, a healthy forest needs to have its overgrowth and undergrowth cleared out, to prevent a more destructive future blaze. This is the more common way the metaphor of fire is used in the Bible—not as an element of torture, but as a purifying force. For example, see Malachi 3:2–3 (NRSV): "For he is like a refiner's fire and like fullers' soap; he will sit as a refiner and purifier of silver, and he will purify the descendants of Levi and refine them like gold and silver, until they present offerings to the Lord in righteousness." (The same kind of language is

used in Isaiah 1:25, 43:2, and 48:10; Zechariah 13:8–9;
Psalm 66:10; Luke 12:49; and 1 Peter 1:7 and 4:12–13.)

If you read the prophets, you will be led through many of
the same stages that any of us go through as we grow up spiritually. In much of their writing, we see early-stage moral responses, full of threat and retribution, as in this passage from
Zephaniah:

> How bitter the sound of the day of Yahweh,
> the day when the warrior shouts his cry of war.
> A day of wrath [*dies irae*] that day,
> a day of distress and agony,
> a day of ruin and devastation. . . .
> I am going to bring such distress on them
> that they will grope like the blind. . . .
> On the day of the fire of his jealousy,
> all the earth will be consumed.
>   (Zephaniah 1:14–18, JB)

This angry, judging spirit animated the Catholic funeral
mass through the Middle Ages and beyond, into the many
funerals I witnessed as a young altar boy. The organist pumped
out the dour and haunting melody with threat and abandon.
She knew it by heart, as I am sure we all did. To this day, many
evangelicals seem to love the word *wrath* in much of their
music. (One wonders how much the reformers reformed us!)
For some reason, we seem to be attracted to threat, no matter
what creed we profess or which group we belong to.

But if you stick with the prophets, you can watch them
progress through various stages of bargaining, conviction,
epiphany, deeper God experience—followed by extended passages of further threat, seductive promises, warnings, and fear—

until they lead you toward and through their own needed deconstruction and into their eventual reconstruction. The old *dies irae* refrain of Zephaniah has, by his last chapter, morphed into something else: "Yahweh your God is in your midst, a victorious warrior. He will exult with joy over you, he will renew you by his love, he will dance with shouts of joy as at a festival" (Zephaniah 3:17, JB). How can this be the same man?

Perhaps prophets (both the true ones and those often referred to as false ones) are mentioned in the Bible to teach us how *not* to do prophecy. False prophets, or poorly stated prophecy, can teach us that half right often passes for right but is often truth's most dangerous counterpart. Truth without love is not transformational truth. Truth from a cruel heart undoes its message. Already in Deuteronomy, a false prophet is described as one who confuses his own truth with God's truth. He is rightly called a "diviner of dreams" (Deuteronomy 13:2). This problem will surely never cease being a problem, but the text immediately gives us a clue for discernment: "Your God is testing you to see whether you indeed love the Lord your God with all your heart and all your soul" (Deuteronomy 13:3, NRSV). The answer is almost too simple.

It seems to be a journey of refining the real message, fire by fire, until we reach a final state of joy and hopefulness. This is the clear trajectory of human life. All of us, prophets included, usually must do it wrong, or partly wrong, many times before we can do it right. It cannot be any different, as a good parent knows.

A good example is the book of Habakkuk, written around 600 B.C. You must endure three full chapters of the prophet's railing and raging until you get to the final three verses, where you can join him in exulting and dancing: "with hind's feet on the high places" (Habakkuk 3:19, KJV). It seems that once

Habakkuk had cataloged the people's wrongdoing and fully appreciated Yahweh's might in coming forth "to save your own anointed" (3:13), he pivoted to praise.

Some scholars call the final three verses Habakkuk's "Great Nevertheless": "Though the fig tree does not blossom, and no fruit is on the vines; though the produce of the olive fails and the fields yield no food; though the flock is cut off from the fold, and there is no herd in the stalls, yet I will rejoice in the Lord" (Habakkuk 3:17–18, NRSV).

Frankly, I think you could describe every one of the prophets eventually yelling "Nevertheless!" after all their raging and convicting.

You cannot read the prophets as if each verse offers a moral example that each of us should follow. Many verses tell you, in effect, what *not* to do. If you quote or follow the prophets in their immature stages, you might end up eating your children (Jeremiah 19:9), firebombing the temple, and meeting a God who is mainly known for his wrath, vanity, divisiveness, pettiness, and petulance (Ezekiel 13). More likely, these verses depict our untransformed self *speaking as if it were God* (which is exactly how the untransformed self likes to speak). You must stay with the text and follow the prophets' progress toward the full word of God.

Only *the whole narrative* of any book of the Bible really deserves to be called inspired. The prophets do eventually arrive at the full picture, but if we do not teach and use such a spiritual or historical-critical approach to our reading of the Bible, we should not be surprised when more and more thinking people give up on Christianity and our willful ignorance about how literature works—which too often is what we substitute for faith. As Catholics used to say, "Grace builds on nature." It does not defeat or overcome nature. That is akin to the philosopher Ken Wilber's helpful direction to learn to "transcend and include."[3]

The prophetic texts end up being lessons on both the purification of message and the purification of method, too. Just like us, none of the prophets seem to begin converted. Isaiah was too anti-temple, Jeremiah projected his own emotions onto God, and Amos might have just enjoyed being a contrarian. *We can only learn great things gradually, it seems!*

Saint Paul says it better: "For we know imperfectly, and *we prophesy imperfectly,* and only when perfection comes will the imperfect come to an end" (1 Corinthians 13:9–10, emphasis mine). This is true for all people, in every age. Paul is saying that teachers and prophets change and grow up, learning by their own mistakes, as Paul famously did himself. This should be the big message that we call *conversion* or *repentance*—and we should remember that it is seldom, quite seldom, a one-time affair.

If we're trying to understand how God moves in the world, searching questions will do us so much more good than firm answers. Jesus and Paul almost force us to ask questions by not covering all their bases as a modern scholar would do. This frankly creates major problems for the cynical postmodern student who is trained to expect answers—and answers with fitting arguments. Almost no biblical writers suffer from such a bias, so let's go a little further.

A METHOD FOR READING THE PROPHETS

This is what I recommend. Read each prophetic book through once. Then reread it and mark it up, looking for the pattern I've described. You might do it like this:

- Historical narrative (most of text): Leave unmarked.

- Response of threat, rage, and retribution: Highlight
  in red.

- Passages of inner conflict and early awareness:
  Highlight in yellow.

- "Suffered-through-to" response (the word of God):
  Highlight in green.

We have created generations of good people who use the
red and yellow verses as if they were inspired, mature statements. But if you read them closely, you will begin to see a
pattern I have long taught about the way we progress as human
beings: from *order* into what seems to be *disorder,* and finally
reaching some kind of *reorder.* Jeremiah, for example, starts as
a "true believer" with his dramatic account of being called by
God (order), but when his work as a prophet makes him unpopular among his people, he goes through major resentment
toward God (disorder). Only in the later chapters, after the
Israelites return from exile, does he break into freedom and
joyous conviction (reorder).

Without this self-correcting path, we all become Narcissus,
falling in love with our own image in the water. Those who
love order need to be humbled by the experience of holy disorder. Those working through disorder need the insight of
reorder, plus a major respect for some basic order (the true
meaning of a conservative), and any new reorder (which progressives love) will soon need a further disordering. It is the
natural flow of grace, for both our individual lives and the lives

of our institutions. The prophets tell us that we can and even must trust this cycle of living and dying.

Without this growth process, most of us believe our first presented order is all there is. This is why we have so much immature religion. What we learn early in life, with the mind of a four- to six-year-old, is just to get us started. We first need the ark and the horrible flood to be literal, but when we act as if this is the main point of such stories, it puts us in an untenable and even absurd position. Where did Cain and Abel's wives come from, for example? Did the whole earth really speak the same language before the Tower of Babel? Are "all Cretans liars" (Titus 1:12)? "Now that I have become a man," Paul says, "all childish ways must be put behind me" (1 Corinthians 13:11). Such passages are a shout-out and a demand for an adult Christianity, rather than the version that sentimentalizes faith at the childish level.

We must know that our formulas and group consensus will never change the world—or ourselves—in the ways that the prophets and Jesus demand. Unless we learn how to study the prophets as a rite of passage into adult religion, I do not think their writings and insights will be of much use.

Jesus gave us a rather clear code for authenticity: "By their fruits you will know them" (Matthew 7:15–20). So let's always look for the fruits of the Spirit in our entire use of the Bible: "love, joy, peace, patience, kindness, goodness, trustfulness, gentleness and self-control" (Galatians 5:22–23, JB). Without such fruits showing themselves, it is me talking, not God. When these fruits are evident, we are talking as one.

"Blessed are those who weep," Jesus says in Matthew's gospel (5:4). Yet we can never mandate tears; we can only allow them, encourage them, and join with them as they soften our soul. Tears encourage us to move forward not by shame or guilt (although there is such a thing as good guilt and needed shame), but by sadness and empathy. The tragedy is in this world, not the next. I believe this is the worldview of the Jewish prophets. What sounds like cynicism and despair about our tragic human reality ends up being utter optimism and satisfaction about history in general and the soul in particular.

CHAPTER 2

Amos: Messenger to the Collective

"I was no prophet and did not belong to any
brotherhood of prophets," Amos told Amaziah the priest.
"I am a mere shepherd and a dresser of fig trees.
Yahweh took me and said, 'Go, prophesy to the people
of Israel.'" (Amos 7:12–15)

The prophet Amos lived in the eighth century B.C. in a small town in Judah called Tekoa. There he scratched out a living as a herdsman and a pruner of trees. His prophecies emerged from neither a formal education nor a family position nor any priestly role or inheritance, but from his foundational perspective as a peasant. Those at the top tend to believe things are the way they are for good reason, but the poor know in their bones that things are not as they should be.

Amos does not initially even claim the title of prophet, as you see above in the chapter-opening quote. You would think his contemporaries would have written him off as an uneducated naysayer, but he was nevertheless a very important voice in Israel, even as he largely criticized the Israelites and others. Most scholars believe he set the tone and manner of a writing prophet and was accepted as such by historic Israel. He showed other prophets how to do it and gave them permission to publicly criticize their own society.

God called Amos during the reign of Jeroboam II (786–746 B.C.), at the height of Israel's greatest territorial expansion and prosperity. Many Israelites interpreted their success as a sign of God's special favor. But Amos saw their society for what it was. He preached against the people's transgressions, their complacency, their reliance on military might, their injustices in social dealing, their immorality, and their shallow piety. He was particularly harsh in criticizing those who squeezed lives of luxury out of an unjust system: "Listen to this word, you cows of Bashan, living in the mountain of Samaria, oppréssing the needy, crushing the poor, saying to your husbands, 'Bring us something to drink'" (Amos 4:1). All of this, of course, put him in conflict with the religious authorities. They expelled Amos from the royal sanctuary and commanded him not to prophesy there again. But he did not obey. He returned to Judah and wrote down the essence of his public preaching, which we have in the book of Amos.

This prophetic culture-smashing, or "bias toward the bottom," as I call it, was largely unrecognized in the West for most of the next three thousand years. Our bias, in our society and in our churches, has invariably been from the top and toward the top. We liked kings and bishops much more than we even noticed layfolk, women, and herdsmen. The common people were not seen as important or influential, despite all that Jesus taught us about "the little ones." That this has been the case shows the unfortunate lack of influence of the Hebrew prophetic mind on religion in general—and Christianity in particular.

The management guru Peter Drucker was famous for saying, "Culture eats strategy for breakfast." In a similar way, I believe that culture eats religion for lunch. By that, I mean our beliefs are determined much more by our dominant ways of life and our surrounding cultural influences than by what we say we believe religiously. In every country where I have taught, it was culture that was running the show far more than religion. The Roman Catholic Church, for example, is far more Roman and parochial than catholic. It is universal in its geographical spread but usually quite provincial and ethnic in its concrete manifestations. We can see this in the unique art and moralities of each Catholic area. Until very recently, artists in Anglo countries were embarrassed at nudity, while Germans and Italians reveled in it. Law is actually expected to be obeyed in English-speaking Catholicism—especially Church law. For Italians, it is just a vague suggestion. (However, it's worth noting that the hookup culture of American youth proceeds at Catholic universities just as much as it does at the Ivy League universities, as far as I can tell.)

Every viewpoint is a view from a point, and we had best know our own. Where you start largely determines the questions you ask (or don't ask), the trajectory you set, and the goals you hope to achieve. Truth does not appear like an apparition of low-hanging fruit in a celestial garden. It always comes wrapped in the society and historical moment that produced it.

This is as true of the prophets' writings as it is for us. Each one of them is situated in a historical moment that is crucial for understanding them. Theoretical truths about the authority of the priesthood or the unfairness of taxes must always be seen in the context of their moment, their society, and their audience. Otherwise, we will interpret their texts in a vacuum, or through our own limited lens, which can lead to misunderstanding—or worse. This was how we arrived, sometimes for a span of centuries, at self-interested interpretations that allowed us to justify prejudice, slavery, exorbitant wealth, and whatever else we preferred. Or, more commonly, we read the whole thing in terms of our private journey toward salvation. When we lose the bias toward the bottom, it's often because we never got on the biblical trajectory to begin with. We were far more Egyptians and Babylonians, Romans and Greeks, than enslaved Hebrews seeking liberation.

Theoretical truths that touch no one deeply are hardly truth at all. Yes, truth is universal and absolute, but it must *show itself in a specific context*. Amos, for example, sequentially names the violence and aggression in "the three crimes, the four crimes" of the cities of Damascus, Gaza, Tyre, Edom, Ammon, and Moab (1:3–2:3). While the text doesn't specify what those "crimes" were, we can assume that Amos's original readers would have been intimately familiar with them. Note that these are the surrounding neighbors of Israel and Judah, so we are not talking about the Jewish covenant here, but more likely universal human values and rights like loyalty and compassion. A true prophet names evil wherever it is festering.

Amos, like other prophets, does not stay forever in his initial anger and threat of punishment. Instead, he transforms his anger into generative, creative energy. After his judgments, warnings, and threats, which take up most of chapters 1–4, we see him moving toward a plaintive sadness in chapter 4:6–11, repeating five times that the people have failed to respond to Yahweh's outreach: "Yet you never came back to me." Here again is the "divine pity" showing itself. He sounds disappointed more than angry at this point, and, surely enough, he breaks into praise several times: "For it was he who formed the mountains and created the wind, reveals his mind to man, and makes both dawn and dark, and walks on the top of the heights of the world—Lord, the God of Hosts, is his name" (Amos 4:13). Amos grows into a mystic poet right before us, balancing out the initial anger of the pruner of trees with the reverence of a fully realized prophet.

EVIL IN THE COLLECTIVE

A second lesson that we draw from Amos, besides his bias toward the bottom, is that he issues his prophecy to the collective rather than to individuals. Even when he singles out the temple priest Amaziah and the king Jeroboam for criticism, they are stand-ins for the two elite groups (priests and rulers) that Amos implicates as part of the corrupt power system. The prophet's judgments are clearly directed at the group, the culture, the collective, the society. Amos knew that most collectives are content to locate evil among individuals. But there is little value in placing our attention merely on a handful of bad actors. Culture and systems are what create the large-scale evils that threaten us—such as poverty, war, and ecological devastation. Religion must address collective evil. Nothing will ever change if we merely convert, imprison, or judge "bad guys."

That is why, though Jesus healed individuals, he simultaneously critiqued the systems that made them need healing. In fact, the best way to interpret most of his healing stories is to look at the whys. Why was a man chained in the cemetery (Luke 8:26–39)? Why were the women Jesus loved so often adulterers and prostitutes (John 8:1–11)? Why has a woman with chronic bleeding given all her money to doctors (Mark 5:26)? If you read these stories as if Jesus is only performing miraculous medical cures, you might think "Wow!" for five seconds. But when you ask why the healing was needed, you have a whole new way of seeing what needs to change, which is invariably the bigger power structure: the institutionalized evils that no longer look evil; the "structural sins," as Pope Francis calls them; or even the collective unconscious, which is often better exposed by art, music, cinema, and theater than it is by preachers.

Amos judges, critiques, and makes promises and threats to many, many collectives. It is a long list: the settlements of Carmel and Damascus, the house of Hazael, Aram, Gaza, Philistia, Tyre, Phoenicia, Edom, Teman, Bozrah, Ammon, Moab, Kerioth, Judah, the Amorites, Egypt, Assyria, Samaria, Gilgal, the house of Israel (many times throughout), Kaiwan, Calneh, Hamath, Gath, the house of Joseph, Karnaim, Arabah, Beersheba, the temple shrine at Bethel, the "tottering hut of David" (9:11, a sarcastic insult), "the remnant of Edom and all the nations that belonged to me" (9:12, JB), and many more. Note that he does not limit divine judgment to the people of Judah and Israel, but directs his prophecies to neighboring nations, who are also under Yahweh's dominion. We need to follow the same pattern today, as leaders around the world did in the Universal Declaration of Human Rights, adopted by the United Nations in 1948.

This concentration on the collectives changes our moral focus entirely. If we do not recognize that evil first and foundationally resides in the group, we will continue to search out, condemn, or perhaps forgive the "few bad apples," thinking that will take care of our problems. But too often, sins we condemn in the individual are admired, or at least given a cultural pass, at the corporate level. Consider some of the contradictions in our own culture, for example:

> Killing is wrong, but war is good.
>
> Greed is wrong, but luxury and capitalism are ideals to be sought after.
>
> Pride is bad, but nationalism and patriotism are admirable (never in the Bible, however).
>
> Lust is wrong, but flirting and seduction are attractive.
>
> Envy is a capital sin, but advertising is our way of life.
>
> Anger at our neighbor is wrong, but angry people get their way.
>
> Sloth is a sin, but wealthy people can take it easy.
>
> Murder is wrong, but easy access to guns is a right and duty.

You can see how we got the sense, shared by many, that we are living under an utterly conflicted morality. Even "capital sins" such as greed and ambition are no longer even critiqued at the individual level, but seen as virtues.

The view from the bottom helps us escape this human tendency. I have learned from a lifetime as a preacher that even a slight critique of capitalism is totally unacceptable in American pulpits. It can be intuitively and freely understood, however, in the barrios of Guatemala, or the lower-middle-class Mexican American parish where I preached regularly until Covid, because their viewpoint is from the receiving end of capitalism's damages. Those who benefit from capitalism, or other dominant systems of power, will often assign virtue to rare, distant individuals called saints—and even then only after they die. We must learn to see virtue as involving some form of giving back to the community and society, not just privatized "purity."

The church has been trying for centuries to save individuals while ignoring the corrupt system in which those individuals operate. God, by definition, deals with the whole, but our egos keep us lost in the small parts that we think we can control. This is why all those millions of individuals who walked the aisle to repent at the Billy Graham crusades did not add up to a nonviolent Mississippi, or a decrease in lynching in Alabama, or a reduction in poverty in California.

My point here is that the prophets approached evil from an entirely different perspective. (See "A Good Summary," page 161.) Amos called out what he termed the oppressive "cows of Bashan" (4:1) instead of just criticizing one anecdotal woman living in the lap of luxury while the poor starved. The prophets, far ahead of their time, learned that it is social sin that destroys civilization and humanity: global warming, war, idealization of immense wealth, celebrity worship, the pursuit of fame and fortune, immense and growing income inequality, a denial of common truth, and on and on. They attacked hidden cultural assumptions more than they did the people caught up in them.

Religion and God, almost by definition, are meant to keep us living in the utterly big picture, the generative and generous state of mind that Jesus called the reign of God. Yet the only real sins we seem to agree on are the sexual ones—and even those, not so much. Jesus, you can see when you read the Gospels, is not much concerned about sexual issues, for example, except as matters of justice and honesty. Even the concept of "social justice" has been misunderstood and malformed by many Americans today. In comfortable countries, the large middle class now shares the perspectives that were historically only those of the privileged and the elite. We have been co-opted with just enough comfort *not* to feel the pinch that most of the developing world feels every day.

The Hebrew prophets found their truth not in books and laws, but in questions of love at its most unsentimental and mature level. Amos's emphasis is clearly *against* temple priests, kings, and luxury, and *for* the common people and justice. I wonder if that's why we Christians know almost nothing about Amos. His message is culturally incompatible with our modern individualistic values, and with our perennial tendency to keep our commitments and responsibilities socially harmless. Do the following pronouncements sound anything like what you hear in your Catholic, evangelical, or mainline church, for example?

> You, Israel, have sold virtuous men for silver,
> Poor men for a pair of sandals,
> You trample on the heads of the ordinary people,
> And push the poor out of your path. (Amos 2:6–7)

> See what disorder there is in Samaria,
> See what oppression is found inside the palaces
> > of Egypt.
> They know nothing of fair dealing,
> they cram their palaces full by harshness and
> > extortion. (Amos 3:9–10)

> I hate, I despise your feasts,
> I take no pleasure in your festivals. . . .
> I reject your burnt offerings,

I refuse to look at your sacrifice of fattened cattle.
Let me hear no more of the din of your chanting,
No more strumming on your harps . . .
Just let justice flow like water
And integrity like an unfailing stream.
   (Amos 5:21–24)

These words from Amos make you think that God intended a very different meaning for society and divine worship than what we now have. Justice, most of us believe, is when we send bad guys to jail! We imagine that we can point out the few who get caught and that then we can think of ourselves as a fair society. But we don't dare convict the whole system of massive injustice and deceit. Maybe we are refusing to carry both guilt and responsibility? Taking responsibility for the common good is the more important moral mandate. And that is exactly where the prophets began. When the common good is the focus, preaching is not about imposing guilt and shame on individuals, but about giving vision and encouragement to society. Perhaps that is why Jesus's most common metaphor for the end times was a wedding banquet, not threats of hellfire and punishment.

What history has needed is a positive and inspiring universal vision for the earth and the people of God. Harping about individual sin and criminal convictions might shame a few individuals into halfhearted obedience, but in terms of societal change it has been a notorious Christian failure. Such an emphasis has backfired because it was not founded in a positive love and appreciation of the good, the true, and the beautiful in the world or in creation. Our shaming of human beings has simply produced an ocean of blowback from folks who already think they are unworthy. Negative energy feeds on itself, but positive energy evokes a positive vision.

So what is Amos's positive vision? When you read the way he ends his prophecy, you can see that the rewards and rejoicing are very much based in this earth and this world. Isn't that what a shepherd and pruner of trees would understand?

> Harvest will follow directly after plowing,
> the treading of grapes immediately after sowing,
> when the mountains will run with new wine and
>   the hills will flow with it.
> I mean to restore the fortunes of my people Israel,
> They will rebuild their ruined cities and live in
>   them,
> plant vineyards and drink their wine, dig gardens
>   and eat their produce.
> I will plant them in their own country, never to be
>   rooted up again,
> out of the land I have given them.
>   (Amos 9:13–15, JB)

There is so much earth-based positivity, human joy, and consciousness of God's love in these statements. When you "let justice flow like water and integrity like an unfailing stream" (5:24, JB), there is little time left for guilt about all the petty so-called sins that came to preoccupy us for most of Christian history.

Radical unity with God and neighbor is the only way any of us truly heals or improves. Perhaps that is why Alcoholics Anonymous continues to make such an enduring difference in people's lives, while serving as a prophetic critique of Sunday, go-to-church Christianity. AA insists on personal responsibility for woundedness, the inner experience of a Higher Power, and some kind of ongoing small-group practice. The whole package of healthy religion, you might say.

By his final verses, Amos sees God as more merciful and more compassionate, even as he continues to lament Israel's foolishness and failures:

> That day I will re-erect the tottering hut of David,
> Make good the gaps in it,
> Restore the ancient ruins,
> And rebuild its ancient ruins. (Amos 9:11)

Amos is inaugurating a revolution in our understanding of how divine love operates among us. This is no longer retribution or punishment, but a full reordering. It is such divine extravagance, a philosophy of *love them into loving me back,* that sets the pattern for all the prophets to follow. He represents a strong and clear movement away from retribution and punishment to what will become a new covenant of restorative justice that we will see worked out in Isaiah, Jeremiah, Ezekiel, and, of course, in the life of Jesus. This changes everything, or at least it should.

CHAPTER 3

A Critical Mass:
The Secret of the Remnant

The surviving remnant of the House of Judah shall bring
> forth
new roots below and fruits above.
For a remnant shall go out from Jerusalem,
and survivors from Mount Zion.
The jealous love of Yahweh Almighty will achieve this.
> (Isaiah 37:31–32, JB)

Over and over in the Old Testament, we see that Yahweh works slowly and humbly to reform any society, starting from the edges and the bottom. This can be seen in a few major examples: the inaugural story of God freeing the Hebrew minority from enslavement in the Egyptian empire; the young David killing the giant warrior Goliath (1 Samuel 17); Micah's prophecy that the Messiah would come from "the smallest of the clans of Judah" (Micah 5:1). It is the consistent biblical theme of themes. The victims are the victors. I am not sure how explicitly the prophets understood this seeming divine strategy, but they certainly learned to work inside of littleness, failure, and rejection from a nonresponsive audience.

In this way, the holy nation—the authentic *qahal Yahweh* (the gathering of the people of God)—emerges by a divine winnowing process. The whole group never gets the message, but a smaller group (the "remnant") carries the love and hope of restoration forward after each purification (that is, after the trials and tribulations the people endure). This seems intentional on God's part. Power distorts truth, so God plants and develops it at the edge, where the power-hungry least expect it. The truth will always be too much for everybody, but God seems content with a few getting the point in each era. The God of the prophets is very patient and very humble, although a cursory reading will not usually reveal that.

This tradition of the remnant is central to the whole Bible. God's message and messengers—and often the hearers—all tend to be outliers to "the way everybody thinks." Thus, when we respect the loved and rejected outsider, the "little ones" become the indication that we are on a tangent of divine love and not just our inherited and natural love of family, sameness, greatness, and ego advantage. Jesus teaches the same concept when he says "when two or three are gathered in my name, I am there" (Matthew 18:20). Such a statement, just as real a promise as any presence in the Eucharist, would make no sense if it were not preceded by Hebrew remnant theology.

I would venture so far as to say that if we had only learned this one message, we could have avoided much of the suffering of human history. Centuries of religious wars could have been prevented if we had sought the truth at every edge instead of in glorified institutions, such as my own Catholic tradition's impossible notion of the "one true church" that God has preferred and blessed.

Throughout Scripture, Yahweh's willingness to continue to work with "the few who get it" forces Israel to constantly rethink its own theology of salvation. It becomes a token of God's own faithfulness: "In your midst I will leave a humble and lowly people; those who remain will seek all their refuge in Yahweh" (Zephaniah 3:12). The "remainder" becomes a standing symbol of how little it takes for God to stay with us. Yet those who are often called the "chosen" or the "elect" are chosen not because of God's actual favoritism toward them, but because of their radical trust in God's universal, nonpunitive, and unconditional love for them. How else does one understand Jesus's flabbergasting teaching to his disciples: "Unless you change and become like little children you will never enter the kingdom of heaven" (Matthew 18:3). Either this is naïve teaching or Jesus knows something that most of us still do not know or appreciate. God uses all of us, but only a remnant seems to enjoy this stewardship consciously.

God is saving all of history and all of humanity, but only with the direct, conscious help of a faithful few. I am sure prophets tried to widen this circle of the faithful, as all preachers hope they are doing. But the amazing thing is that they taught us how to be content when that faith response does not happen. (I have wondered if this partly explains why Jonah acts surprised, even disappointed, when the Ninevites do respond to his warnings.) I suspect they knew they had to explicitly model such faithfulness if they wanted others to learn it themselves.

I find it striking, for example, that Yahweh commanded the prophet Hosea to marry a prostitute (1:2) so that he could

learn that love and mercy apply even when love is not recipro-
cated. Hosea is told to keep loving his wife, Gomer, despite
her many adulteries, so he can understand at a bodily level
God's love for Israel in her unworthiness. Here Yahweh needs
to get Hosea to literally put some skin in the game, to see what
both love and adultery feel like! Divine largesse will always be
too much love for the masses and those who are convinced of
their own innocence, but that does not mean divine love is not
at work—and most effective for those who widen their nets
and open their hearts. God can love the whole, and the whole
can enjoy God's mercies (as we do every day!) without consciously knowing it. It just increases our joy and effectiveness
tenfold when we do.

This revelation of the remnant is the clear opposite of our
notion of majority rule, authority rule, Christendom, or even
"one person, one vote." In a very clear way, it presents an utterly counterintuitive theme that a humble minority is always
the critical stand-in for God's big truth—and the group
through which God is working change. In nineteenth-century
America, for example, the Black enslaved understood the liberating gospel, while the white minority created an exclusivist,
imperial belief system that could barely be called Christianity.
This privileged form of white Christianity survives to this day
and is still racist, materialistic, and largely preoccupied with the
small self. God loves them totally, too, but they don't show
many signs that they enjoy it. You meet two or three who
allow themselves to be loved and chosen in every church, and
you have the feeling they are keeping the whole group sane.
This is how remnant theology works in practice.

We might think of the remnant as what scientists call a
"critical mass": the amount that activates the energy in a
chemical reaction—or, in this context, the energy in the larger

group. The critical mass in biblical theology is always the small, "edgy" group that carries history forward almost in spite of the whole. Think of Noah and his family in the ark; the youngest and forgotten son David becoming king; the barren wives Sarah and Elizabeth, each giving birth to a special child late in life; the twelve outlier fishermen being called as Jesus's disciples instead of anybody from the capital city temple team.

Without this ego-defeating tactic of the critical mass, Christianity always becomes what we now call civil religion, where the powerful assume they have the authority of the truth, simply because they are in power. Popular thinking is given the presumption of orthodoxy. The prophets, however, consistently laugh at the supposedly normal and parody the so-called successful. "I wither the green tree and make the withered tree green. I have spoken and I will do it," Ezekiel records Yahweh as saying, summarizing Israel's history from God's perspective (Ezekiel 17:24).

The normal power systems of our world worship themselves and not God. That hardly needs any proof at this point in history, after we have witnessed so many corrupt institutions in both church and state. For that reason, prophets almost never hold official positions, like that of a king, priest, or elder. However, neither do they dismiss the proper roles that kings and priests play in maintaining the basic order of society. A good example is when Jesus on several occasions (e.g., Luke 14), after healing people completely outside the temple system, still tells them to follow the rules. After he cures a leper, he says, "Go show yourself to the priest and make the offering prescribed by Moses, as evidence for them" (Matthew 8:4, JB). Elsewhere he critiques priests loudly and publicly, but in the end he does not set up an antagonism. Such honoring of all parts reflects the remnant's avoidance of a dualistic and puritanical worldview. He does not cash in on another group's failure, as I would be tempted to do. Everything finally belongs.

Throughout history, we have waited for the charismatic prophet to come together in the same person as the institutional leader, but it happens only rarely, as with King David after he submitted to the prophet Nathan. Later in history, we saw more leaders who managed to perform both roles at once: individuals like Thomas Becket, the archbishop of Canterbury; Queen Elizabeth of Hungary; Mother Katharine Drexel of Philadelphia; and Óscar Romero, the archbishop of San Salvador, all of whom were institutional people who nevertheless operated at a critical distance from their church role to be faithful to their own call. In our time, Pope Francis is an amazing and most rare example of one who can operate as both high priest and high prophet (not without his critics, however).

Often, prophets emerge from the rank and file, paying the dues of their group so they can later critique it and not be seen as outsiders. They have shown themselves to be not iconoclasts, but legitimate reformers from within. They are in fact "exciters" of the critical mass, always wise beyond their years and living by higher values that are foreign to their contemporaries. They seem to lead just by living their lives and do not need any honorific titles or initials after their names.

THE REMNANT TODAY

In just about every society, those who are not rich, famous, or at the top carry an undue stigma—some degree of guilt and shame for their lesser status. The unspoken assumption is, *You are surely wrong and at fault because you belong to the wrong subgroup, have no wealth, do not work hard enough, or have not made it to the celebrity list.* And yet the Bible breaks this pattern by preferring the barren wife, the forgotten son, the enslaved Israelites. Those in the remnant carry the mostly hidden truth forward despite—or probably because of—their rejected or marginal status. It is a loser's script leading from Sarah to the Israelites and all the way to Jesus, but neither group—Israel or Christianity—ever really wants to play the part. We preferred Zionism and Christendom.

Despite this revelation of the remnant, those in the larger group almost always blame the ones they consider "less than" for whatever they are lacking, a tragic tendency we now call "blaming the victim." Failure in almost any form is considered "your own fault" in any upwardly mobile or fully capitalistic society. "The poor" live with a double indemnity. They are blamed not only for their own personal failings but also in many cases for the larger group's problems and sins. But the prophets refuse to scapegoat anyone by always giving their own group a good thrashing first and foremost. They turn the dial 180 degrees, shaming the victors and oppressors by pointing out that their apparent success is really a form of failure. The Bible was not supposed to be used to idealize ego and empire, as most humans throughout history have tried to do. As Jesus makes clear in his very first sermon, his work is "to bring the good news to the poor, to proclaim liberty to captives, and to the blind new sight, to set the downtrodden free." (In this passage from Luke 4:18, JB, he was quoting Isaiah 61:1–2.)

His teaching sets in motion what I would like to call the biblical pattern of "anti-scapegoating," or preemptive self-criticism, a learned capacity to see your own shadow. We see it in Jesus's overarching humility. He remained personally a prophet, working outside the priesthood and the aristocracy, but he did not let that make him into a rebel or an iconoclast. A thin line, it seems. The intended effect was meant to be monumental and new for history. But it did not take root. The Roman empire began to take control of the gospel as early as A.D. 313, and soon the world was being divided into groups of sinners and saints, the worthy and the unworthy who deserved to be scapegoated.

We still have not recovered from this inability to live this original reforming genius of Jesus and the prophets. Most of the time we find ourselves happily on the side of the successful, of ego and ill-gotten comfort, rather than the side of truth and justice. Nor did we stop blaming the "other": believers versus unbelievers, Christians versus Jews, men versus women, normative versus "queer," the rich versus the poor. These patterns of thought have destroyed much of the transformative power of the gospel, for individuals and even more for cultures. In our time, someone else must always be the problem, especially the other race or the other political party, even when the fault line is clearly running through our own country, group, ethnicity, or gender. Conspiracy theories are woven out of thin air in hopes of convicting someone else, rather than us and our group.

I would ask you to open up any prophetic writing on almost any page. Rather than scapegoating others, the prophets consistently call out the fault, the blame, the bad people as the Israelites themselves. This makes the biblical text quite revolutionary and exceptional—and so different from the habits of our own era. *The Hebrew prophets critique their own group first, and only then does that give them enough clarity to properly critique others.* This pattern of prophetic critique is the norm, and it probably explains why the prophets have never been emphasized in synagogue and church preaching to this day.

Listen to this, priests,
attend, House of Israel,
listen, royal household, you who are responsible
    for justice. . . .
They [the Israelites] are entrenched in their
    deceitfulness,
And so I am going to punish them all.
I know all about Ephraim, Israel has no secrets
    from me. . . .
Yes, you have played the whore, Israel has defiled
    himself.
. . . a prostituting spirit possesses them;
they do not know Yahweh. (Hosea 5:1–4, JB)

Most of the time, one just cannot talk this way to their own group without losing all cachet. But the prophets were able to do so because there was a kind of social agreement within Israel to tolerate and expect the prophets' provocations, no matter how much they hated them. As much as their society often rejected their messages or sought to punish them, there was also an understanding and acceptance of the prophetic role because the prophets were precisely those assumed to be speaking for God. We no longer enjoy such an assumption. In fact we oppose it!

There are even frequent mentions in the Bible of "bands" or "companies" of prophets. We no longer have such a thing, and thus we do not raise up many who can use the role maturely. There are no institutional protections for prophets in most churches. The Orthodox and Catholics do occasionally benefit from their hierarchical model when bishops personally protect members on the edge from the hostility of the masses. Bishop Guido of Assisi, for example, was famously praised for surrounding the naked Saint Francis with his cape when his father and family came to assault him. Because of this, Francis told his followers to always have a "cardinal protector." I have personally enjoyed that gift, both in Cincinnati and Santa Fe.

The final line in the text above from Hosea is the clincher: The people's fault, their core mistake, is that "they do not know Yahweh." *They* do not recognize how God has been patient and forgiving with them, nor have they learned how divine love operates. They still presume, as we all do in the absence of a vital spiritual experience, a rather universal reward-punishment logic. But for the prophets and their students, God's unconditional love is the hallmark, the ideal, and the model for all human behavior—reaching its epitome in the teaching of Jesus.

DIVINE-HUMAN LOVE IN HOSEA

Hosea uses love and marriage as striking metaphors for the divine-human relationship. Some of his images even have erotic undertones: "I am going to lure her and lead her out into the wilderness and speak to her heart" (Hosea 2:14). Speaking of this relationship with Israel, Hosea says, "I shall betroth you to myself forever, I shall betroth you in uprightness and justice, and faithful love and tenderness. Yes, I shall betroth you to myself in loyalty and in the knowledge of Yahweh" (Hosea 2:19–20, JB). Marriage has the possibility of mutuality and reciprocity and intimacy, whereas the parent-child relationship carries a very different power dynamic.

But too many are *too attached to their own power and violence* to let God be the spouse that Hosea describes. Instead, for them, God can only be the angry and judgmental deity they see in Scripture and in their churches and neighborhoods. Only mystics and those who pray from the heart escape this trap, it seems to me. They have met the infinite mercy and stopped counting, measuring, and weighing themselves and others. They know these acts are meaningless. The rest of us keep trying to compute and settle for polite civil religion instead of *presencing* and participating in what is always immeasurable. The prophets would surely say God loves the weighers and measurers too, but they enjoy the message much less (as you can often see on their faces) and are much less able to pass it on. We might say they are called but have never allowed themselves to be chosen.

Think of the poor scribes and Pharisees in the New Testament, who try so hard to be right and dutiful but seldom win the praise of Jesus. "You shut up the kingdom of heaven in men's faces," Jesus tells them, "neither going in yourselves nor allowing others to go in who want to" (Matthew 23:13). I personally believe that spiritual teachers who are filled with warnings and cautions operate out of a deep, pervasive sense of absence, searching always for some justification that God is here and on their side. Once you have been met on the inside, you know there *is* an inside because it has met you there. In the presence of divine love, your cautions and warnings all fall away as unnecessary and unhelpful.

Divine love becomes for the prophets the standard for God's relationship with God's people, and it will be taken up by Isaiah, Jeremiah, Ezekiel, the Song of Songs, and the majority of Christian mystics down to the present age, evolving into Sacred Heart spirituality in its many forms to this day. But Hosea is the first prophet to clearly move the tradition from law to heart, from the parent-child dynamic ("I was like someone who lifts an infant close against his cheek," 11:4), to spousal intimacy ("I will go back to my first husband [Yahweh], I was happier then than I am today," 2:7), to what sounds like a kind of universal betrothal to life itself ("I will make a treaty on her behalf with the wild animals, with the birds of heaven and the creeping things of the earth," 2:18–20). This is a God in love. A God who wants to show us how he loves by sending Hosea back to Gomer, his unfaithful wife, again and again. He made Hosea learn how such love feels in his bones—and it seems he did.

This unique foundation in physical love was strangely laid out in Genesis 17:1–14, when male circumcision of the foreskin became the sign of God's covenant with Noah. (*Shouldn't the rainbow have been enough?* every man must have said!) This is admittedly a crude metaphor for the contemporary mind, but note that it quite precisely names that the male organ of symbolic force and dominance is what needs to suffer some radical surgery. I personally believe that the Jewish initiation rite of male circumcision, and *not* female, was an early, radical visible and physical critique of the false uses of power and domination we call patriarchy. It is archetypal, I think. Throughout the prophets, a circumcised foreskin was expanded to a circumcised heart (as in Deuteronomy 10:16 and Jeremiah 4:4), with the prophet Jeremiah using a daring symbol to condemn the entire Jewish people: "Plainly their ears are uncircumcised. They cannot listen" (Jeremiah 6:10). They needed a circumcision of the ears and the heart because they were not listening to, nor had they experienced, a truly felt love. The same has been true of every generation since.

The prophets often reached for grating, shocking metaphors that would move transformation from the realm of ideas alone to the realm of body, mind, and spirit. Once the male body can be transformed, becoming a physical symbol of the covenant, then perhaps our religions and societies can also be reformed. But laws and prohibitions usually win our attention because they are more clearheaded and quantifiable than anything to do with love, intimacy, and surrender. Forgiveness and mercy are just too fluid and messy—unearnable!

We like to know exactly where we stand with the Almighty at any given moment. Obedience and disobedience are much clearer indicators of a worthy God relationship than "You shall love Yahweh your God with all your heart, with all your soul, with all your strength" (Deuteronomy 6:5). We never know if we have done that yet, or even where to begin, and so most people would rather just stick with the Ten Commandments and know that the law is on their side. At least we know whether we did something or not. Yet the words of Jesus ring in our ears, words he learned from his Father but surely would have confirmed by studying the prophets: " 'You shall love the Lord your God with all your heart, and with all your soul, and with all your mind.' This is the greatest and first commandment. And the second is like it: 'You shall love your neighbor as yourself.' On these two commandments hang all the Law, and the Prophets" (Matthew 22:37–40). Mark goes further, saying that these two great commandments "are far more important than any burnt offerings or sacrifice" (12:33)—and more important than any other divine or church rules.

The Jewish prophets never reached the same critical mass as the ordained elders, scribes, and teachers of the law, but they were the ones who held on to the purified, mystical message of Judaism and Christianity, and thus kept it from disappearing. A minority within a minority, they taught the refined and actual message of love of God and neighbor as one, which is full religious transformation.

There are plenty of prophets among us now in every church

and society, and it is vitally important that we listen to them, support them, and protect them. Ofttimes, they are not formally aligned with religion, yet they are deeply influenced by its deepest values, like the "Heroes" CNN celebrates each year, or those who work tirelessly for women's rights, children's rights, and human rights without much notice or reward. I deliberately do not begin to name them specifically, because there are so many of them. Like the Suffering Servant of Isaiah, they:

> Do not cry out or shout aloud,
> Or make their voice heard in the streets,
> But faithfully they bring true justice
> Refusing to be wavered or crushed,
> Until true justice is established on earth.
>   (Isaiah 42:2)

They are not just a critical minority, but a largely *hidden* critical minority—the remnant and a critical mass, which we are all and always invited to join and protect.

Of course, such prophetic people do cry out and shout aloud and try to make their voices heard today, but it is always in the service of true justice and love, not the current popular, politically correct issue. Dorothy Day is an outstanding example of someone who would not cooperate with public opinion. She opposed the U.S. entry into World War II and refused to participate in the anti–nuclear war drills of the 1950s, when resistance was illegal and almost unheard of. When the air-raid sirens sounded, she appeared quietly and publicly with other protesters in a public park, holding a sign that quoted Pope John XXIII: "Why should the resources of human genius and the riches of the people turn more often to preparing arms . . .

than to increasing the welfare of all classes of citizens and particularly of the poor?"[1]

Civil disobedience is often the prophets' unique platform as unofficial speakers of the deeper truth of nonviolence. Dorothy Day refused to be rallied into a national state of sacralized violence. Such people don't want or need a pulpit, although they surely deserve one. And we need them to move us toward limiting and critiquing even "good" wars, such as World War II. Otherwise war becomes massive violence and righteousness, destroying both sides.

Like the people of ancient Israel, we must remove the obstacles that keep us from recognizing these truth-tellers, the critical masses that are speaking in our times. In fact, we must let God circumcise both our ears and our hearts so that we can hear them fully. They are not seeking fame or fortune, or they would not be prophets. They will never be mainstream; they will always be a remnant. But it is their message that they care about, not their reputation or their comfort. They are supremely orthodox to those with equally circumcised ears and hearts, and probably fools to almost all the rest of us. This will not change.

CHAPTER 4

Welcoming Holy Disorder: How the Prophets Carry Us Through

One reason that the radical reforms of the Catholic Church's Second Vatican Council (1962–1965) did not fully take hold at the time, and even up to this day, is that the Catholic Church was doing quite well, by most measures, in 1965. Parishes were well attended, there was no shortage of quality priests and nuns to staff Catholic institutions, and worshippers worldwide still possessed a strong group identity. Many saw no obvious or felt reason to fix what did not appear to be broken.

Yet a minority of leaders felt a strong need to "throw open the windows of the church and let the fresh air of the spirit blow through," as Pope John XXIII put it. Vatican II sought to open those windows by reforming liturgy, preaching, returning to Scripture, emphasizing the role of laypeople and relationships with other faiths, and even changing the physical layout of churches. Officially, those changes were the new order, but there has been plenty of disorder in their implementation. Latin Masses kept us with a sense of mystery and superiority. Our criticism had remained firmly aimed outward at Protestants and pagans and modernists. "Why fix what was not broken?" traditionalists shouted, and still shout even to this day. Only those of us who grew up in the old church know how broken it was on so many levels.

This pattern plays out within all kinds of institutions. Reforms rarely move directly from the existing order to a new order automatically or by a single positive insight. The old order has to somehow show its disorder, its shadow self, its injustices, its wrongness. Then there must be a period of disorder, a fertile time of searching before a new order can be found. The rule must reveal some exceptions to the rule before any reordering will be sought, trusted, or allowed—and even then all things human will still reveal themselves as incomplete.

Religion in its healthy forms gives every culture a method of survival through all of this change process, some form of learning how to "die early," so that you can keep moving when the world seems—and is—always chaotic and tragic. The summary word for that method is *trust*—the kind of trust that occasionally lives in darkness, like Jonah in the belly of the sea monster. We need trust in some initial order (good parenting and healthy religion), but also trust in disorder when it eventually shows itself (good prophets help us here), and then trust in the new, livable, and ever-changing home base called reorder (love, community, and friendship).

For our purposes here, I call the starting place, the first order, the "priestly rule." These are the rules and governing personalities that hold our worlds together as normal and regular. Many call this "establishment thinking." It can take military form, royal form, philosophical form, tribal form, or some religious form, but without such primary order, we would all go crazy. We need some point of reference, even if just to push against. (In my book *Falling Upward*, I wrote that the construction of this order is the important task of the "first half of life.")[1] Recently, this innate reverence for order took cosmological form in the near-ecstatic response to a total solar eclipse. *There is order and predictability*, people seemed to shout.

But when personal or historical disorder shows itself—and it always does—we will begin a necessary period of critique, change, or rebellion. I am calling this disorder the "prophetic rule." It is always opposed and resisted, and thus needs wise protectors and guides and the strong ego structure that the preceding order provides. An Indigenous person who believed the myths of his or her culture probably had a stronger sense of self than today's postmodern person, who denies all real or operative transcendence.

As I wrote earlier, the Old Testament frequently mentions prophets, and even bands or "schools" of prophets, which filled this need for dissent within the system. Yet few cultures have had training for these crucial dissenters, apart from the Jewish people. If such internal, legitimated critics are not allowed, let alone encouraged and trained, history will only move forward at the cost of blood and heartbreak. Growth will not be organic or inclusive; instead, it will be largely exclusionary and punishing of whatever is in that moment considered the problem. Negative energy, or critical energy, does not usually become constructive or useful unless some prophetic types enter the scene early in the process of change.

I founded the Center for Action and Contemplation (CAC)

here in Albuquerque, New Mexico, in 1987 because of a growing sense that we needed to educate people to be truth-tellers who are *inside and effective critics of* religious institutions, without becoming negative or cynical themselves—a loyal opposition, as we call it today. We knew that there must be a way to make room for prophecy—what Paul called the *second* most important spiritual gift for the building up of the body of Christ (1 Corinthians 12:28, Ephesians 4:11–12). Prophets move us beyond uncritical groupthink. Every group and every movement have their shadow sides. We need trained seers who are neither co-dependent on the religious system for their identity (such as clergy) nor seeking to make a good name for themselves.

The CAC's message became a balancing act between action and contemplation—forming contemplative activists and engaged contemplatives—in the lineage of the mature Hebrew prophets we have been discussing. I am so glad we put this goal in our title: Center for Action *and* Contemplation. It holds us in a classic and creative tension, in which *and* is the most important word. Action comes before contemplation because you do not have anything to contemplate until you have acted in the world and recognized that the real issues are difficult to resolve—tied up in deep motivations like identity, power, and money. Often what you think is the issue is not even the issue at all.

Prophets, as we have seen, occupy an entirely different role from priests and ministers. (I take up this distinction at length in "A Good Summary," page 161.) And we surely need all of them! There is little evidence that most priests are change agents—or even desire to be, except in an in-house, churchy sense. Instead of truth-telling, they are more concerned with maintaining order and orthodoxy within the group. Yet they are offered a ready bully pulpit, a free audience, and a decorated stage every week. I think we now need a new kind of seminary that includes training for prophets who educate for holy disorder—a breaking down of the expected, the tried and true, the false, the ways in which we are not faithful to the gospel—even if doing so upsets and disrupts. Up until now, we have been too interested in lots of "unholy order." There is really no reason we can't have priestly prophets and prophetic priests. (It is no wonder the Old Testament word *priest* was seldom used in the first three centuries of Christianity, and *minister, disciple,* and *overseer* were preferred.)

True prophets will guide us into, hold us inside of, and then pull us through to the other side of what will always seem like disorder. The more you have bought into any kind of absolute and necessary order, the bigger a dose of disorder you will need. A rule follower, for example, might need to confront a situation where their rules just don't work—and be honest about it. Those who hate gay people might need to have a family member, friend, or someone they care about come out as gay before their perspective can change. Biblical literalists need to encounter contradictions in the text that cannot be easily reconciled. A self-affirming pastor needs to meet people who expect truth from scientists more than clergy, and so on. It is in and through such conflicts that we come to third-way thinking and acting, moving beyond the argumentative dualistic mind to the creative contemplative mind where our ego is not steering the ship.[2]

This is how we find creative balance, both as individuals and in our institutions. Certainly not by punishing the "early adopters" and turning them into external critics. Critics can be loyal believers, too, and it is the prophets who show us how.

THE QUALITIES OF A PROPHET

Up until now, we have had two thousand years of Christian "priests," a title, as I just mentioned, that neither Jesus nor Paul applied to Jesus's apostles or disciples. But no one was sought, or tolerated, as a prophet after Jesus himself ascended from this world. In fact, one hardly hears the term unless we are looking to the ancient past. After years of study, I see the following ten developed qualities in would-be prophets:

- They can *honestly explain* the problem within the solution (rather than denying or ignoring it, whatever it is) and thus move toward *truly transcending* it. The bishops of the Second Vatican Council, for example, tried to take this approach in the 1960s, but they did not have the pedagogical skills to pull it off. They were accustomed to the old command structure doing the job. They modeled in all sixteen major documents how to use Scripture intelligently and faithfully for a church that had not taught Scripture very much or very well. It was, and is, our Achilles' heel in most dialogues with Protestants.

- As I mentioned earlier, they are humble enough to have some real detachment from their own opinion and status, because true prophets know the message is not theirs. They are merely being used. I see this in Archbishop Desmond Tutu, in the manner in which he led the Truth and Reconciliation Commission in South Africa.

- They can still love and respect those who have a different opinion. Rare at first, this quality must be trained and formed. Think of the nonviolent teachings of Mahatma Gandhi and Martin Luther King, Jr.

- They do not need to be right, first, or best. Think of Dorothy Day and the Catholic Worker Movement training Christians to live alongside homeless people, rather than serving them as superiors or saviors.

- True prophets will pursue some knowledge of theology and Scripture, for the sake of good initial boundaries. Without education in the history of wisdom, we will only have our own temperament and culture to guide us. We will not think outside our already provided box. Prophets offer us patterns of what we call "alternative orthodoxy"—living on *the edge of the inside* and concerning themselves with right practice more than right belief. Martin Luther King, Jr., for example, was Black, American, and Christian, which best situated him to be both a leader and a critic of American Christians. Remember our previous chapter on the crowd versus the remnant. Positive reform almost never emerges from "what everybody thinks." (See "Seven Themes of an Alternative Orthodoxy," page 167.)

- They have a capacity for some degree of objective thinking beyond their own agenda, ego, and grievances. They have other avenues to truth than just "the Bible says so."

- They are team players and not just lone rangers. They are loyal to at least a couple of communities. Think of Viktor Frankl, the Austrian Jewish psychiatrist who survived the Holocaust and yet still attended both synagogue and Catholic masses with his wife.

- The issue they are confronting is really the issue, and not merely a means for them to achieve power, importance, or fame.

- All in all, they have purified motivations—what Jesus calls "a pure heart"—or, at minimum, some growing ability to recognize when their motives are mixed or their heart is not pure. Think of Mother Teresa and her willingness to keep going even in her "dark nights of the soul."

- They manifest the classic "fruits of the Spirit," both in their person and in the effects of their message. It is hard to improve on St. Paul's inspired enumeration in Galatians 5:22–23: "love, joy, peace, patience, kindness, goodness, trustfulness, gentleness, and self-control." These are fruits that will last, the surest measure that someone is speaking from solid ground. This is probably too Catholic, but I think of the women who founded almost every community of nuns, who succeeded with little institutional understanding or support in a church that just wanted cheap workers. I was taught in elementary school by many such women, many of whom were not theologians but exhibited lots of daily virtue.

No prophet achieves all of these qualities perfectly, but he or she must clearly be moving toward them. They create an absolutely necessary coherence between the medium and the message.

Without those qualities, we see many who are supposedly truth-tellers, yet what they manifest is not the fruits of the Spirit. Many reformers, after all, have been known less for the quality of their love than for the intensity of their zeal. I think of Jonathan Edwards, an eighteenth-century Puritan revivalist and minister whose message to his flock was more about God's anger and fear than about Paul's fruits of the Spirit, as you can see from the title of his most famous sermon, "Sinners in the Hands of an Angry God." We see this in many American politicians today, where their message is largely *themselves and their reelections:* "gongs booming and cymbals clashing," as Paul puts it in 1 Corinthians 13:1. Such booming and clashing has much increased in our age of social media and the memorable soundbite. Intensity must not be confused with truth, either in preachers or politicians, although sometimes it is also needed and helpful.

Most of the prophets surely made mistakes before their message could be refined or even heard, as we see in their unhelpful rage and dualistic judgments. A major assertion in this whole book is that they were angry, even depressed, before they were sad and enlightened. Remember when Paul said that "prophesying [can be] imperfect" (1 Corinthians 13:9) and still be prophecy? Good news indeed.

A divine message can be given more effectively by an actively loving person. I suppose that is obvious. Angry or constantly irritated people present resentful, wrathful messages that only embolden their egos and misdirect the audience into more anger rather than pointing them to the truth of the message itself.

The common biblical descriptor for strident, angry messages is *righteous*. Far from the meaning we normally give that word, the biblical authors are describing everything from the zealotry of youth to a dangerous self-absorption that takes over when passion, rage, and overstatement become one's operating persona. It takes studied and prayerful discernment to know the difference. When is zeal good? When is zeal mere self-absorption or ambition? When, on the other hand, does it show appropriate passion for a big truth? These are the necessary struggles and growth edges for a prophet, I think, and not an immediate sign that they are wrong.

"A PROPHET'S REWARD"

"Anyone who receives a prophet because he is a prophet will have a prophet's reward; and anyone who receives a holy man because he is a holy man will have a holy man's reward," says Jesus in Matthew 10:41 (what I call "the Apostolic Master Class"). But what might that mean? I think a prophet's reward—as well as the reward for those who receive a prophet—is precisely *nothing*, except the telling of the message itself. When you want and need something extra, like fame, money, or notoriety, the truth is already lost.

Jesus is forever purifying his messengers by pulling them outside of the usual reward systems. Saint Francis deeply understood this. It's why he trained his followers to be ministers for the gospel instead of seeing them as ministers for the church. He himself deliberately remained a brother, or friar, and always refused the higher status of priestly ordination. His vow of poverty, first of all, had a social function, situating him and his followers outside of power politics, although for others it later became merely a private virtue, a form of asceticism for

one's own "personal salvation." The Buddha, by his own ad-
mission, made the same mistake. Both of these spiritual leaders
wanted to change culture and not just sanctify individuals by
their "holy beggary." They knew that there had to be a way to
live on the edge of the inside without totally exiting the fold.
They thus *de-idealized* the supposed inside. Buddhism pulled
it off to some degree in many cultures. Franciscanism had
Western capitalism to deal with, and by the thirteenth century
was quickly tamed.[3]

Prophets are surely the most obvious example of Jesus's
instruction that you should bless those who cannot reward you
in return. When you throw a party, he said, do not ask *those
whom you fear might repay you.* But when you throw a party,
invite those who cannot pay you back! You will be fortunate because now you will look for your rewards on a whole different
level (Luke 14:12–14, my paraphrase). Prophecy is the least
licensed and rewarded of any of the charisms or ministries. In
fact, it is more likely that a prophet will experience persecution
and misunderstanding, rather than perks or career advance-
ment. As the final beatitude says: "Blessed are you when they
insult you and utter every kind of evil against you because of
me. Rejoice and be glad, for your reward will be great in
heaven; this is how they persecuted the prophets before you"
(Matthew 5:11–12).

To be used as a prophet or to follow a prophet's lead should
profit you nothing! Otherwise the role and the message are
corrupted. A prophet is not a weathervane seeking reelection,
but the free-blowing wind itself (John 3:8). If a prophet is put
on any kind of career track or staff org chart, his or her whole
role and mission will be distorted or even destroyed. Forgive
me, but I think we took the prophetic role away from most

priests and bishops when we accustomed them to praise, costumes, salaries, and promotions.

Keep in mind that prophets speak prophetically out of an
obedience to God—*or they are not speaking prophecy.* Obedience is, first of all, a form of *listening* to God (*ob-audire* = to
listen to), and only then can there be prophetic speaking. Hear
the prophet Jeremiah in the throes of this struggle: "I used to
say, 'I will not think about him [Yahweh]. I will not speak in
his name anymore.' Then there seemed to be a fire burning in
my heart, imprisoned in my bones. The effort to restrain it
wearied me, I could not bear it" (Jeremiah 20:9). Or consider
Ezekiel's words: "Say to those who make up prophecies out of
their own heads . . . The Lord Yahweh says this, Woe to the
foolish prophets who follow their own spirit without seeing
anything" (Ezekiel 13:2–3, JB).

False prophets are precisely those who confuse their own
agenda with God's agenda. They are the most common form,
it seems. On the other hand, those accustomed to obeying the
inner spirit have learned to practice co-knowing (*con-scire* = to
know *with* consciousness). They embody and teach shared
knowing *with* God by not claiming their thoughts as their
own, as hard as that is to say!

For me this is a central concept. I have learned this principle well, I hope. I take frequent forty-day hermitages, and
these retreats have become my primary listening stations over
the years. Without them, and without the many public plat-
forms I was given to teach and preach, I could never have operated prophetically, if I ever did. There is no one-way
prophecy, no speaking without listening or listening without
speaking. The flow must go both ways, or it is not divine flow.

One must have a regular sense that the core of one's own

thoughts comes from beyond one's own cogitating and rea-
soning. I know this is dangerous, and there is no shortage of
would-be spiritual leaders claiming that their ideas come from
the divine, often hiding behind "the Bible says" or "the church
says." Look for humility, love, and detachment in the speaker.
If those elements are not present, be careful and rightly doubt-
ful. A prophet does not need to push the river of her ideas *too
feverishly*, because she knows the source of the river is beyond
her.

Prophetic speech is never arbitrary or just interesting. It is
always *necessary* speech—the truth that no one is asking for, or
even expecting, but that desperately needs to be said for the
field to be widened and deepened. We all know people who by
one remark open up the conversation. That is what prophets
do. It is often said that when prophets stir some level of con-
troversy and pushback, their message might just be the gospel.
Protocols and procedures are usually easy to agree with, but
not prophetic speech, which comes from a different level of
consciousness. For those who know nothing about deep intu-
ition, it feels like switching engines. And you can't switch if
you have never accessed this mind before. It is never indepen-
dent or autonomous knowing—although in the first stages of
pushback, one might well fear that it is. Prophets must have
asked themselves, many times, *How do I know this is not just my
idea?* They have learned to be their own devil's advocate.

This is another reason why too many superficial payoffs will
corrupt the prophetic ministry. It's why Saint Francis, the
founder of my order, made so much of humility, simplicity,
and the vow of poverty. He tried to situate Christian ministry
on a whole new level outside the transactional economy of his
time—and ours. This has had limited success. Even among us
Franciscans, "stipends" soon became salaries, expected and

mandated in the same way we do with tips in the United States today. Be careful when institutions "hire" you as a form of domestication! My membership in the Order of Friars Minor, commonly called the Franciscans, made it unnecessary for me to seek gainful employment my whole life. Few enjoy such freedom.

You must do prophecy, the spreading of love and holiness, *for free*—or your message will not have the energy and power of the gospel. I know spiritual teachers who refuse all forms of payment and insist on working pro bono. Others require that all donations are given to a third party so that the exchange itself is not cheapened. I experienced this mostly in Asia among begging monks and at free guesthouses run by monasteries. Having worked with staff in any number of institutions over the years, I cannot help but notice that unpaid board members and volunteers are often more committed to the real mission and message than the paid staff are. Maybe you have seen that, too?

If prophets *must* be untied from payment in order to ensure the freedom of their soul and its message, one must at least question how true it might be for the rest of us involved in spiritual work. Some Buddhists and Cistercian guesthouses seem more practiced in giving "free retreats" and welcoming students on a donation basis than many of us who have made spiritual teaching our livelihood.

Jesus, the ultimate prophet for many of us, said, "You received without charge, give without charge" (Matthew 10:8, JB). Giving without charge—and not expecting any pay—has been a gift of my Franciscan community and my solemn vow of poverty. When I joined the friars in 1961, we still had what we called a "syndic," an accountant of sorts who received and paid out all money so that we could live free from even having to think about it or even touch it. (*What a luxury!* many of you are surely thinking.)

I am surely not poor in any practical sense, but the Franciscans and my parents, who grew up during the Depression in Dust Bowl–era Kansas, made me quite happy with the satisfaction of doing the work and delivering the message—"a prophet's reward." As a priest and teacher, I was able to do this when called for fifty years, knowing that I had received my own education and formation without any charge. Without such sincere gestures, the gospel loses all ability to change the soul's equations, to challenge our all-encompassing emphasis on wealth and begin to teach *a gift economy.*[4]

The prophet's goal, then, is always to create an alternative world based in Spirit and not in mammon. Most never would have imagined that God and divine law could be the alternative to what is "normal" or customary. Thus, it is no real surprise that Jeremiah describes himself as a deconstructor of impure systems more than a teacher of ethics: "Each time I speak the word, I have to howl and proclaim: 'Violence and ruin!'" (Jeremiah 20:8, JB).

You see, prophets seldom preach peace and prosperity, as we're accustomed to hearing from political candidates and most people who seek public notoriety. Instead, "From remote times the prophets who preceded you and me prophesied war, famine, and plague. . . . But the prophet who prophesies peace can only be recognized as a prophet when his word comes true" (Jeremiah 28:8–9). Why? Because things are always falling apart and the prophet's job is to illustrate that *catastrophes eventually have to happen and we must allow them to happen.*

This profound thought reminds me of the oft-quoted conclusion to the Buddhist Heart Sutra in Sanskrit: "*Gate, gate, paragate, parasamgate.*" (The word *gate* is pronounced with two syllables, *gah-tay*.) It can be translated as "Gone, gone, utterly gone, all has gone over to the other shore." It is almost the Buddhist form of saying "Amen"! If "all" has gone over to the other shore, then the purpose and goal have been fulfilled. It has run its course; it has passed through death to life ("the other shore"). I often repeat these words to myself as a personal consolation and an expression of radical acceptance in the face of all the world's woes and tragedies. It demonstrates the allowing at the heart of both Buddhism and the Jewish prophets.

I remember when Eckhart Tolle, whom I consider a prophet, gave an interview on 9/11 entitled "Even the sun will die." The prophet is never shocked by death—even the death of what we might think immortal. And this is exactly my point: The prophet can best hear and be heard during times of holy disorder (what mystics have called "darkness" and what I call "liminal space"). When our "sure things" fall apart, the prophets show how they were built on illusion and power to begin with, and not finally real.

This message of necessary disorder is very hard for overly ordered people and superpatriots to believe, but it is a crucial presence in our world. If we allow it to do its work on us, this prophetic disruption can open up our accepted sense of what's possible, making room for evolving people, for exceptions to our normal ways of doing things, and for something genuinely new to happen. Remember, every time God forgives sin, he is saying that *relationship matters more than his own rules.* Think about that. *Forgiveness honors disorder while still naming it disorder.*

At first, we resent almost anyone who appears to be "making an exception of themselves" by critiquing the normal and even the holy. Yet prophets help us to realize that they are *re-*

vealing what was always true anyway—but remained hidden or denied. They are telling us, like an exorcist driving out a demon, "Show yourself!" They bring our shadow selves out for all to see, and on that count alone will be usually unpopular.

Priests are not prophets as such. Their concern must be to keep the existing system going without usually asking, "Is any of this changing people on the level of consciousness, truth, or love?" But prophets keep the priestly systems "good" and honest by starting with a sincere inner life of contemplation *and* a gradual purification of motive. Ritual and routine alone do not normally achieve such changes in our imagination and character on their own, but confrontations with our own woundedness and darkness often can.

I wonder if this explains, at least in part, the Bible's total obsession with sin. Much of life is, in fact, disorder—and we seem to need constant reminding of this uncomfortable truth. Thus, *we need both priests and prophets. We need order and then critique of that order, and then further resolution, which I call reorder.* When I talk about reorder, I do not mean jumping straight from the status quo to a glib reorder without first exposing ourselves to the refining fire of suffering, dying to self, and inclusion of the shadow. Ezekiel, as we will see in chapter 9, had to let himself be considered foolish, eccentric, a bit deranged, before he could begin to deliver most of his messages. Pope Francis recently praised comedians for doing just this! Yet Ezekiel could not allow himself to be put so deeply into the disorder category that mainline Judaism could not hear him. A high-wire act, I think. I'm not even sure it worked, because, as we will soon see, both Judaism and Christianity failed to get Ezekiel's, Jeremiah's, or Job's restoration message.

When criticism is not tolerated or encouraged, the proud, deceitful, and power hungry will invariably win out. Every institution needs designated, positive, and affirmed whistleblowers, or the shadow always takes over and the problem is never included in the resolution.

ENCOURAGING HOLY DISORDER

How do we begin to form radical traditionalists and reformers for the church? How do we create schools for prophets? How do we train people to be so loving that they can be *effective insider critics* of religious institutions, or what we call the loyal opposition, without becoming negative or cynical themselves? Licensed and beloved critics are what we need! There must be a way to make room for this second most important of the charisms for the building up of the body of Christ (1 Corinthians 12:28). Only then can we hope to move beyond competing denominationalism and, frankly, pride.

Every group, every movement has its shadow side, and always will. There must be those who make the rest of us lovingly aware of what we cannot see. I think of Pope John Paul II's visit to Nicaragua in the 1970s, when Mercy Sister Theresa Kane and Nicaraguan priest Ernesto Cardenal courteously but clearly chided the pope to his face. They both pointed out, in effect, his inconsistency in presenting himself as a liberationist while appointing far-right bishops and cardinals throughout the world. The pope was not amused. It also surprised the media world—although pleasantly, and for very different reasons. John Paul II was not used to being corrected, and the media just loved bringing down a powerful person.

Even Jesus faced criticism from a Syrophoenician woman,

after she asked him to cast a demon out of her daughter. When Jesus equated her—triply marginalized as a pagan, a foreigner, and a woman in a patriarchal society—with a dog, she humbly rebuked him: "Sir, even the dogs under the table eat the children's crumbs" (Mark 7:28, Matthew 15:21–27). He allowed her to play the prophet for him and disagree with him publicly. And what did he say back to her? "You have great faith!" (Matthew 15:28). He accepted her holy disorder, apologized, and made amends.

It is counterproductive to our own gospel message to keep excommunicating and dismissing our would-be reformers: people like Origen of Alexandria, Peter Waldo, Giordano Bruno, the Spiritual Franciscans of the thirteenth and fourteenth centuries, Jan Hus, the Beguines, numerous women founders of religious communities, Martin Luther, and legions of progressive theologians like Leonardo Boff and Jon Sobrino in the twentieth century. Without a positive internal program for ongoing reform, we will just keep calling forth rebels, iconoclasts, and overreacting heretics to guide reforms. You could say that Pope Leo X made a heretic out of Martin Luther by refusing to hear any of the truth of his ninety-five theses nailed on the door of the Wittenberg cathedral. Instead, he insisted that Luther renounce all of his writings while Luther was still asking for an amicable discussion. After that, there was no one to cry foul—except perhaps Erasmus of Rotterdam.

Reformers from without are too easy to dismiss and easy to exclude. Someone must be trained and blessed for the prophetic role of official devil's advocate from inside the community. Then they no longer work for the "devil" but for the angels of light—and cannot easily be dismissed. Then holy disorder can bear fruit and become a new source of an order founded on God's love for everyone. No exceptions.

CHAPTER 5

Jeremiah: The Patterns
That Carry Us Across

J eremiah is rightly considered one of the major prophets. Not only is he prominent in the Old Testament, but Jesus and the authors of the New Testament quote him extensively. His influence even extends to nonreligious settings. A *Jeremiah* is someone who pronounces cosmic judgment and warns of the need for repentance and change. A *jeremiad* is a type of bitter lament at unrighteousness or a prophecy of doom, typified by the sermons of Puritan preachers that cataloged the people's sins and warned New Englanders of God's coming wrath. But the actual Jeremiah is much more than that.

Though most scholars find the book of Jeremiah to be a collection of manuscripts without much chronological or biographical order, it is generally agreed that this author taught in two crucial periods in Israel's history: before the Babylonian exile (his call was in 626 B.C.), warning the people it was coming, and during the exile, telling them to trust it. He was active until the destruction of the Jerusalem Temple (586 B.C.), and concluded that all hope for the future would come precisely from those who had passed through such a purifying journey.

In his anger stage, Jeremiah condemned the people of Israel for forsaking Yahweh and instead worshipping the idols of Baal, a Canaanite fertility god. The people had broken their covenant with God, Jeremiah warned, and they would soon suffer famine, foreign conquest, plunder, and captivity in a land of strangers. Jeremiah's prophecies so enraged those who did not want to hear them that they plotted to kill him and put him in prison. Eventually, they threw him in a cistern and left him to starve, but he was rescued by Ebed-melech, an Ethiopian eunuch in the king's house who pulled him out with the help of three men (Jeremiah 38:7–13). Here we see the emerging pattern that God's people are invariably rescued by those on the edges themselves. After this, Jeremiah was told that Ebed-melech must be protected from his enemies, too (Jeremiah 39:15–18).

From his dramatic call as a young man to his many years of prophesying about upcoming and needed suffering—and being persecuted for it—Jeremiah lived the prophetic pattern fully and is rightly thought of as a forerunner to Jesus. He began in anger, as all prophets do, but he did not stay there, moving into lamentation and slowly tiptoeing into praise. Midway through the book, while having no real-life evidence for such praise, he shouts, "Jerusalem shall be my theme of joy, my honor, and my boast, before all the nations of the earth" (Jeremiah 33:9, JB).

In this way, Jeremiah was always out ahead of his people. In the introduction to the Jerusalem Bible, the translator goes so far as to call him "the father of all that was best in Judaism," largely because of his comprehension of the nature and implications of the new covenant that God was inaugurating during this period of crisis. He needed a lot of cachet to spread such a message among people who never imagined anything more than the existing covenant. Yet his teachings about God's infinite love are as challenging to us today as they were for his contemporaries. We would all do well to listen.

THE RELUCTANT PROPHET

Jeremiah's early resistance to God's call has earned him the moniker "the Reluctant Prophet." Who would not be reluctant when given the burden of delivering a constant, urgent message of violence and ruin (Jeremiah 20:8, JB) to people who in no way wanted to hear anything other than happily-ever-after stories? He starts off hopeful and inspired, with God assuring him that he will be protected, but it is not long before his jeremiads about the hypocrisy and sin of Israel make him a feared and maybe even unwelcome figure. Chapters 11, 14–18, and 20 provide some of the most agonizing and colorful writing in the whole Bible, as the prophet pleads his case before God:

> You have misled me, Yahweh,
> and I have let myself be misled,
> You have overpowered me; you were the stronger.
> I am a daily laughingstock, the butt of every joke.
> Each time I speak, I must howl violence and
> destruction!

I used to say "I will not think about God anymore,
I will not speak in his name anymore,"
Then there seemed to be a fire burning in my
    heart.
I am weary with holding it in and I could not bear
    it. (Jeremiah 20:7–9)

God must have been extremely real for Jeremiah to write in this way. Living in secular, materialistic America, it is hard to imagine having such intimacy and honesty in one's experience of faith. Yet it feels trustworthy when we witness it in Jeremiah. In human history, only Jacob's wrestling with the angel and the testimonies of medieval Catholic mystics like Teresa of Ávila match the intensity of Jeremiah's struggle with the divine. But I suspect it will resonate, especially with those of us who have struggled with life's purpose or fought through depression and doubt.

As a young man, I so identified with Jeremiah and his call that I chose it as the first reading at the first Mass I celebrated in 1970:

Now the word of the Lord came to me, saying,
Before I formed you in the womb I knew you, and
    before you were born
I consecrated you; I appointed you a prophet to the
    nations.
Then I said, "Ah, Lord God! Truly I do not know
    how to speak, for I am only a boy."
But the Lord said to me, "Do not say, 'I am only a
    boy'; for you shall go to all to whom I send
    you, And you shall speak whatever I
    command you. Do not be afraid of them, for
    I am with you to deliver you, says the Lord."

> Then the Lord put out his hand and touched my
> mouth; and the Lord said to me, "Now I
> have put my words in your mouth. See
> today I appoint you over nations and over
> kingdoms to pluck up and to pull down, to
> destroy and to overthrow, to build and to
> plant." (Jeremiah 1:4–10, NRSV)

I still relate to it deeply, especially when I'm in what feels like a perpetual critical mode toward church and state. It would be so much nicer to just go about my life as a happy Franciscan, but prophets need to live *on the edge of the inside* if they are to speak from a proper perspective—definitely not in the comfortable center, but also not outside throwing stones without empathy for the full situation. Most of us settle for a more defined position: fervent insiders, rebels against any belonging system, or too jaded to place our bet anywhere.

Jeremiah certainly started with plenty of anger and warnings of retribution. In chapters 2–7, we find him raging, indicting the people's use of religious worship as a substitute for justice, which places him directly in the lineage of Amos and Isaiah. It is no accident that Jesus later quotes Jeremiah's words directly[1] when he unleashes his own form of holy disorder in the temple: "Do you take this Temple that bears my name for a robbers' den?" (Jeremiah 7:11, JB).

Note how, even as they berate the hypocrisy of their religious leaders, neither Jesus nor Jeremiah actually denies the sacred, which is our much bigger problem today. As a culture, we question any practical need for sacred space or inherent value to prayer beyond civil religion. We might bow our heads during a moment of silence or take our newborn child to be baptized, but these displays are often performative, an attempt to be civil more than really worshipful. It is hard for us all to admit how utterly disenchanted much of our society has now become. We question whether there are any real sacred spaces, people, or objects.

Do not confuse prophets with modern secularists. Instead of denying the sacred dimensions of life, they *transpose* the sacred from place to person and create a universal availability and access to God—from rote ritual to sincere prayer, from rocks to a living presence. They never throw out the sacred. Jesus builds directly on this by "speaking of the sanctuary as his body" (John 2:21): a place not for the buying and selling of God, but a "place of prayer for *all* the people" (Mark 11:17). The people's lack of recognition of this universal welcome is what brings Jesus to tears over Jerusalem: "because you did not recognize your opportunity when God offered it" (Luke 19:44, JB). History has almost always preferred scapegoated animals and people, or nothing sacred at all, to simple prayer to a quite conversational God.

I think we can say that Jesus saw himself as a prophet of the Jeremiah lineage, emphasizing a lifestyle of justice and compassion instead of temple worship. We would do well to remember that today. Christianity, in whatever form it takes, is not about attendance at religious services, proper group-defining rituals, or priestly performances. God does not, as Jeremiah and Jesus preached, desire to be worshipped, or we have a very needy and co-dependent God. Isaiah also advocates strongly for this idea:

> What are your endless sacrifices to me, says Yahweh,
> I am sick of your burnt offerings of rams and the
>   fat of calves.
> The blood of bulls and of goats revolts me. . . .

Who asks you to trample over my courts?
Bring me your worthless offerings no more,
The smoke of them fills me with disgust. . . .
I cannot endure your festivals and your
    solemnities. . . .
When you multiply your prayers, I shall not listen,
Your hands are covered with blood.
Search for justice, help the oppressed, be just to the
    orphan,
Plead for the widow. (Isaiah 1:11–17)

True worship's function is to radically decenter our naturally imperial ego, but too often it devolves into some notion of needed sacrifice, as it did for the ancient Israelites. We drift back into an instrumental religion of necessary payments, deserved rewards, laws, and prescribed liturgies.

Eventually one has to decide, *Am I in love with the metaphors for their own sake? Or am I in love with the thing itself?* Read the book of Job, especially chapters 38–39, where Yahweh describes in beautiful detail the animal and cosmic world as revelations of God by their very mysterious existence. God does not seem preoccupied with staged reality (like formal worship); rather, he creates reality *itself*, in which matter and spirit already operate as one,[2] everywhere and all the time, as in the mysteries of biology and all of the natural and animal world. Our job is simply and daringly to "imitate God" (Ephesians 5:1), and God is nothing if not a doer and an extremely creative creator. It is almost too embarrassing, too easy, and too simple to just keep following and repeating nature's song and dance of praise. Yet this is Miriam's performative prophecy that we see in Exodus 15:20.

So many religious people could be called "defenders of the

metaphors"! They love the bread or the water, but do not go where they point: to the inherent sacrality of quite ordinary things. The blessing that a priest waves over them only uncovers what is always and already there. Yet this confusion is probably inevitable, unless you have the prophetic imagination that recognizes that all religion has to work with is metaphors (*meta* + *pherein* = that which carries you over). They carry us across to mystery itself. But religion often mistakes the metaphors and rituals for Reality Itself. Authentic Christianity must be an utter commitment to reality, as opposed to ritual, or it is not a commitment to God.

The soul surely uses and enjoys well-done rituals—the kind where we are not just affirming ourselves by roles, genders, or sacred words that only some can speak, but also pointing ourselves to the transcendent and to the always-present presence. The question is whether the ritual is pointing to the good, the true, and the beautiful, or pointing to the drama. We should also always look for whether someone or something is being scapegoated in the performance.

REDEEMING THE COLLECTIVE

One of the notable aspects of prophecy that Jeremiah illustrates so well is that he calls on the people, not as individuals but as a collective, to repent and mend their ways, just as we saw in Amos. But Jeremiah does not stay there. He breaks the pattern, offering a vision of redemption that is far more potent than anything we would dare dream up for ourselves.

As I wrote earlier, in Western individualistic thinking, we primarily attribute evil or sin to individual "bad guys," because it assures us that some level of control and containment are possible. Collective evil—such as institutionalized racism, corporate greed, structural homophobia, and gun culture—is almost impossible to adjudicate and, sadly, almost always implicates us! So we just keep looking for obvious bad apples out there. If we can identify those wrongdoers, blame them, punish them as scapegoats, we can carry on living as we did. It also unites society rather well, making it a big payoff for politicians and "high priests," who blame and accuse others as a way of diverting attention from their own misdeeds.

In contrast, the entire covenant between Israel and Yahweh is stated in collective language: "I will give *them* a heart to acknowledge that I am Yahweh. *They* shall be my people, and I will be *their* God" (Jeremiah 24:7, emphasis mine). This is the lasting formula throughout Jeremiah, and indeed the whole Old Testament. The punishments the prophets promised were overwhelmingly in this world (famine, drought, plague, war, etc.), not the personal hell that emerged later in Christian mythology.[3] Bland, shadowy Sheol, or Hades, was neither reward nor punishment, but simply the place of the dead. But Christians projected the worst judgments and punishments on individuals, and into the next world with purgatory and hell. This decision left us focused there, instead of on this world, as we can see in the way we are still ignoring the climate crisis and in our easy toleration for war and racism.

It's notable how the Bible localizes punishment on the earth itself, but not on individual people. There are no names given for the victims of Noah's flood, for example, or for those on whom the fire and brimstone fell in the cities of Sodom and Gomorrah (Genesis 19:24–26). This pattern of corporate punishment—and, perhaps more surprising, corporate grace—is typical of the prophets, and certainly Jeremiah: "Yet *they* did not obey or incline *their* ears, but, in the stubbornness of *their* evil will, *they* walked in *their* own counsels, and looked backward rather than forward" (7:24, NRSV). It is the collective that suffers and the collective that is also rewarded with flowers, rain, and verdant fields (for example, see Isaiah 45:8).

This is a very different way of prophesying than predicting personal doom. Yet such passages as this are so common in the prophets that it could be called the norm: "The wild beasts will honour me, jackals and ostriches, because I am putting water in the wilderness . . . to give my people drink. The people I have formed for myself will sing my praises" (Isaiah 43:20–21).

The Bible is an inspired attempt to write down what reality is saying through nature and history, and only occasionally through personal biography. The continuous storyline is that the joys and disappointments of the visible world are revelations of a less visible one. The less visible one is in control and is ultimately benevolent. Faith is our attempt to recognize and trust such benevolence.

BREAKING THE LINK WITH VIOLENCE

As we evolve gradually toward a capacity for unconditional love and gratuitous forgiveness (just as we do in any lasting friendship or marriage), a huge break must be made in our typical emotional and religious logic. In so many belief systems, and so many countries around the world, our notion of justice requires that all evil be commensurately punished, and all virtue be rewarded. This is our punishment-and-reward system.

Most of us grow up with "win-lose" logic passing for some kind of objective truth. We see this logic in the worlds of sports, debate, war, parenting young children, and even in capitalism, where scarcity and competition are accepted and even celebrated. The ecstatic, irrational cheering that takes place in a baseball stadium or on a trading floor should reveal that we are dealing with something more than the Boston Red Sox or the New York Stock Exchange. We are drawn, especially in the collective, to archetypal premonitions of final victories and final failures. Why else would these contests matter so much to so many, usually without obvious reasons?

Constant success does not teach you much that is helpful in terms of the less visible world. The prophets call our obsession with winning the "mind of empire" and obsessively warn Israel against going there. Our experiences of conflict, though, force us to go inside and find a more durable source of inner worth. This is the continual and constant pattern, revealed in the countercultural clothing that so many of the prophets favored. Jeremiah is instructed to wear a loin cloth but not to wash it (Jeremiah 13:1); Ezekiel is told to take a razor and cut his hair and beard (5:1); John the Baptizer wore a camel-hair garment and ate locusts (Matthew 3:4). They are never "company men." They speak in favor not of holy orders but of holy disorder (pun intended). We have seen such holy disorders throughout history in the rather universal overthrow of kings, the sixteenth-century Protestant Reformation, the Enlightenment of the seventeenth and eighteenth centuries, the hippie revolution of the 1960s, and now the present postmodern collapse of the very idea and importance of truth.

We must first honor the plank of order, next walk the plank that is always disorder, and only then fall into the ocean of infinite everything. At least that is what I continue to say at my wedding homilies. When we are committed to the law of Torah, or basic law and justice, for example, only then can we dare venture into the disruption of the Old Testament's proph-

ets, and trust that we're being led on a great journey. There
must be enough order to contain the disorder, enough authentic conservativism to hold together the scary advance of
history, enough containment to hold a lot of variation. This
very real tension is necessary to make us clarify our thinking,
refine our laws, and stretch our humanity. Paul called this phenomenon "the folly of the cross," where God took the worst
thing, the killing of the Christ-Man, and made it into the best
thing, the very redemption of the world. When we can hold
two such ideas in tension, it breaks down our dualistic mind
and sets us free to move on to reorder.

We can recognize this new order (reorder) when it is *less
violent* and *more universal* than the previous arrangement. Jeremiah leaps toward such a reorder by introducing the unthinkable idea of a whole new covenant (31:31–34) to replace the
old one. Hear Yahweh speaking to him, in a consummate but
seldom-quoted passage from the Old Testament:

> I will not cease in my efforts for their good, and I will
> put respect for me into their hearts, so that they turn
> from me no more. It will be my pleasure to bring about
> their good, and I will plant them firmly in this land, with
> all my heart and soul. (Jeremiah 32:40–41, JB)

Jeremiah has successfully walked us through the trauma of
exile, all the while breaking the logic of vengeance and privilege that we normally use to interpret such events. Instead of
seeing punishment or "winning" as the endpoint of the people's story, he proclaims that Yahweh loves Israel even more
when they sin: "I have loved you with an everlasting love, so I
am constant in my affection for you" (Jeremiah 31:3, JB). This

is an early movement into in-depth healing of trauma, nonviolence, and non-dual thinking:

> I will hasten their recovery and their cure,
> . . . I will let them know peace and security in full
>   measure,
> I will restore the fortunes of both Judah and
>   Jerusalem,
> And build them again as they were before,
> I will cleanse them of every sin they have
>   committed against me . . .
> all these I will forgive, and Jerusalem shall be my
>   joy, my honor, and my boast,
> Before all the nations of the earth.
>   (Jeremiah 33:6–9, JB)

Where did Jeremiah get the freedom and courage to talk
this way? Only God could have provoked such generosity.

Whatever inner experience Jeremiah underwent to transform his theology, it must be allowed to fully transform ours.
It is the movement from external signs of belonging to the
internal "heart" religion (Jeremiah 32:39–41) so treasured by
Jesus. *Let's just move entirely beyond any notion of retribution or
punishment,* he joyously promises, *as the frame for how God's
justice is done!*

This is so hard to conceive of that most of us are still not
there twenty-five hundred years after Jeremiah. Sincerely religious people, trained in forgiveness, exodus, exile, and cruci-
fixion, should be the readiest and most prepared for this full
journey, but up until now that has only been the case in a small
remnant of every group. These are the evolved people whom

we called "saints" and "prophets." Like Job, Moses, Jeremiah, Erasmus, Harriet Tubman, the suffragettes, Martin Luther King, Jr., Protestant reformers, and radical Catholic nuns and priests, they always emerge before, during, and after any big societal event—be it a disaster or a major rearrangement of the historical reality.

After hearing Jeremiah's message of retribution and restoration, the officials were nevertheless disturbed by the logic-breaking truth he spoke. "The fellow," they said, "does not have the welfare of this people at heart so much as its ruin" (Jeremiah 38:4, JB). They threw him into the cistern, "and into the mud Jeremiah sank" (Jeremiah 38:6). Here again we see the common pattern: the new reorder is too much, and many desire to return to the original order, where things that look and talk like a duck are indeed ducks! Only someone who himself has been marginalized or silenced knows how really unfair the rules, expectations, and boundaries of any empire are. Prophets seem uniquely equipped to interpret the law without throwing out the law or the lawgivers.

This deeper, more compassionate grasp of the law seems impossible to the company man! The joiners and the belongers really have no need for grace or mercy; they imagine that they got to "the top" by their hard work, group loyalty, and good behavior ("by following the law"), so they tend not to understand the totally unreasonable and irresponsible concept of grace. This is why groupthink and church loyalty are so commonly substituted for the love of God. Loyalty is actually a form of co-dependency, giving us a warped sense of control and safety, while love is a dive into perfect freedom. Your loyalty could just as well be to General Motors.

Such false logic must be broken again in every new generation. Jeremiah dares to give a revolutionary and even iconoclastic shape to that task: a brilliant and rare combination of radical conservative values with edgy progressive ones—at the same time and in the same person. That is what prophets are good for. This is what Jesus completes and why he is "foretold" by the prophets. A rare miracle indeed!

THE "THREAT" OF UNCONDITIONAL LOVE

The first covenant between Yahweh and Israel appeared to be bilateral: "If you obey my voice and hold fast to my covenant, you of all the nations shall be my very own" (Exodus 19:5, JB). But the new one that emerged in Jeremiah's time was unilateral *from Yahweh's side*: "I will put my law within them, and I will write it on their hearts; and I will be their God, and they shall be my people" (Jeremiah 31:33, NRSV). This dramatic change replaces the earlier order by surpassing it, not destroying it. God forgives undeservedly, even after direct disobedience! This is a love that waits and hopes and desires, working toward surrender and trust. It gifts us a new covenant that we can actually fulfill, just not perfectly or by ourselves. Only God can fill in all the gaps. Henceforth, there is no such thing as deserving or earning anything. All is grace.

Further, humanity's obedience is no longer to be associated with laws and external behavior. Yahweh even offers the unthinkable to our guilt-ridden species: "I will never call your sins to mind!" (Jeremiah 31:34). Jeremiah 31 is frankly a total changing of the guard—and what is guarded is only the human capacity for intimate reciprocal love! As many scholars have agreed, the notion of a God-initiated, unilaterally fulfilled divine relationship is the highest peak of any spirituality, especially since most of us fear, deep down, that we're unworthy of it.

This new covenant prophesied by Jeremiah is what Catholics and other Christians around the world hear weekly, in Jesus's words at the Eucharist: "Drink this cup of the new and everlasting covenant, signed in my blood, and poured out for you" (Luke 22:20). It is deeply unfortunate that the old covenant is so written in our dualistic logic of tit for tat that most Christians remain untouched by this proclamation of a spiritual revolution. We remain content with retribution and vengeance passing for justice. We still appear to say, "The old is good" (Luke 5:39). *Give me that old-time religion!* We would rather stand outside of love than receive a love of which we believe we are not worthy—or have not earned or cannot figure out. In the old covenant, at least we know where we stand, even if it is outside of paradise. We seem to find certitude more comforting than we do trust or love.

I made a personal decision to follow Jesus Christ as my Lord and Savior, many say. Too often, this is understood not as a form of letting go or a recognition of divine grace, but as another ego assertion, in which we're doing all the most important work. When we are preoccupied with saving ourselves, the mind has not moved down into the heart, and our consciousness remains untransformed. As Ezekiel says, "A new heart also will I give you, and a new spirit will I put within you: and I will take away the stony heart out of your flesh, and I will give you a heart of flesh" (Ezekiel 36:26). The "heart of flesh" is not just a transfer into a new group that confirms our specialness and salvation. It is an utterly honest recognition that *I am not the primary "doer" in the world of love. It is being done unto me.* If you have ever been in love, you don't need my convincing in order to know that.

Infinite love is literally too much for most of us to comprehend. We think we know how to love—alone. But how do we know and love together with a "divine another" living within us? The answer is by participation rather than performance—riding the divine coattails, as it were. Most of us think of consciousness as a secretion of our brains, or something we enact by our own willpower, when it is really a jumping on board, a divine flow that we step into, a holy plank that we walk into an infinite but good unknown. Paul's code word for this, his most commonly used phrase, is *en Cristo*. Our whole life, for Paul, is "in Christ," a life of full divine participation with and in the other. Not a private moral endeavor or achievement, but a full communion with reality achieved by surrender to an always-present love!

Many of the students who have come through the CAC's Living School in its first ten years are recovering evangelicals, Catholics, and Mormons who recognized that they were quietly living with a heart of stone and a politics of control, which is really the old covenant. These are usually professional, educated people who have worked toward some level of success within their given field. Yet they have reached a level of awareness and humility that, for me, puts them in the school of Jeremiah. They still love the tradition, have critiqued it in a quite self-demanding way, and have come to love it again in a fresh and life-giving spirit. They are Jeremian-Jesus people, who started in the old covenant and are morphing into the new, as so many of us do in the "second half of life."[4] Fear is less their motive now, and love is creeping in at all levels, almost unbeknown to themselves. Real life has undone them and redone them, as great love and great suffering seem to have done to dear Jeremiah.

In his aloneness and anguish, this prophet saw what a majority still cannot see twenty-five hundred years later. Our refusal to allow ourselves to be loved undeservedly and unconditionally will probably forever be the anguish of every prophet and the burden of every mystic or saint. Jeremiah's scroll of writings was cut into pieces and burned by King Jehoiakim (Jeremiah 36). This is how threatening any new covenant, or any new anything, is to a world already set in full and determined motion.

CHAPTER 6

Unfinished Prophets: Elijah, Jonah, and John the Baptizer

No man born of woman is greater than John the Baptizer, yet the least in the kingdom of God is greater than he. (Matthew 11:11)

My major thesis in this book is that most prophets invariably start with legitimate but righteously dualistic anger at the sins and injustice in the world. As they pursue their calling to teach what they think is God's truth, they confront confusion, denial, doubt, love, and most especially epiphany. Maturing prophets let these experiences change them, allowing themselves to evolve into non-dual and compassionate truth-tellers. But not all of the prophets we read about in the Bible mature in this way. What I call "unfinished prophets" don't evolve and mature but persist in anger, blaming, and accusations. They remain moralistic and judgmental, but without the non-dual mysticism that characterizes a mature prophet—a criterion that will gradually become clearer as we proceed. Not everyone in the Bible is a saint by later standards, but most are people God *can use for some purpose.*

One of these unfinished prophets—John the Baptizer—may surprise you, but I hope you will be able to eventually see why, as Jesus says, "the least in the kingdom of God is greater than he is" (Matthew 11:11). John's purity-code moralism is the common substitute for the mysticism we see in Jesus, a pattern that endures in many, if not most, churches to this day. His baptism is mere "water," a simple outer purification, whereas Jesus's baptism is "fire and Spirit." That is much more about inner transformation and a new consciousness.

John the Baptizer is often seen as the successor of Elijah, another unfinished prophet we'll consider in this chapter. Elijah was a dramatic and violent messenger heralding the day of God's judgment (Matthew 17:1–13; Mark 9:2–13). Elijah and John may have kept growing beyond these stages. We are not sure. After all, the Carmelites consider Elijah their "Holy Father," and it's not for nothing that we speak of *Saint* John the Baptizer. My conclusion is that John and Elijah grew up just like all the rest of the prophets; we just aren't permitted to see all of the stages in the text. We must believe what the Bible says, but often keep an eye open for what it does not say.

These two prophets—along with Jonah, as we'll see—clearly fall short of the reign of God, and yet they still do some of God's work.* Isn't that true of each one of us? A person can operate as a prophet on occasion without being a complete or mature one. There is welcome mercy in this, I think.

Elijah, Jonah, and John the Baptizer behave in ways that art and cinema and even church teachings tell us are typical of prophets, railing against others' moral failures and seeming to

---

* I would say the same about Nahum and Obadiah, but no one ever quotes them anyway!

relish doling out punishment. No wonder that most people do not know how to imitate them, nor would they even want to. I think God must be very humble; if not, he could not act through such fallible humans as all of us. (Note that this builds on what we saw in chapter 5 about God using the "little" and the "poor" in many senses.) This is reminiscent of Paul's reference to himself and his fellow Jesus followers as "earthenware jars" (or "bodies of clay"), a comparison he strikes "to make it clear that such an overwhelming power comes from God and not from us" (2 Corinthians 4:7, JB). I know this to be true personally.

Some never get beyond their shortcomings and shortsightedness, but there they are in the Bible, holding out lessons that we can nevertheless learn from today.

ELIJAH: STUCK IN SPECTACLE

Elijah (c. 875 B.C.) never wrote anything but is presented in 1 Kings as a violent, dualistic man. In 1 Kings 18:20–40, in response to the ascendancy of the cult of Baal, Elijah meets 450 of its prophets and priests in a contest on Mount Carmel to determine which deity is the true God of Israel. On an altar to Baal and another to Yahweh, wood and sacrifices are placed. Elijah says, "You call on the name of your god and I will call on the name of the Lord; the god who answers by fire is indeed God" (1 Kings 18:24). The Baal prophets appeal unsuccessfully for their god to kindle the wood on their altar, but Yahweh answers Elijah's prayers by starting a fire on his altar. Elijah tells the Israelites, "Seize the prophets of Baal: do not let one of them escape" (1 Kings 18:40). He then slaughters them.

I recognize this is a new perspective for most of us, but there is no way we can sanitize these murders. At this point in the story, Yahweh had not yet led Elijah to the top of Mount Horeb (the place where Moses received the Ten Commandments), revealing himself as "a gentle breeze," rather than in the "mighty wind," the earthquake, and the fire (1 Kings 19:11–12, JB). Elijah then stands "at the entrance of the cave" (1 Kings 19:13, JB), covering his face with his cloak, which is brilliant archetypal symbolism for partial knowledge of Mystery.

Prophets who continue to lead (or end) with their rage have only half of the message, it seems. They have the anger but lack the compassion; mere moral positioning and ethical "answers" are not really the work of conversion. Smug people are not really holy people. These unfinished prophets often pass for the real deal because people confuse firebrands, liberals, zealots, and ideologues for those possessing deeper truth. But just because a person is passionate and skilled at gathering crowds does not mean that she or he knows *how or where to lead people beyond that.* As Jesus says, "many false prophets will arise, and lead many astray" (Matthew 24:11, NRSV). In our times, it is common to confuse articulate passion with prophecy when it is often simply untransformed anger that will not change anything in the long term or lead us anywhere good. Passion and prophecy are not the same thing. Contrarians are often just contrarians.

It is not just the "what," or content, of the message that is inspired but, more important, the "who." Who is doing the speaking, and why? What is the full energy of the message in substance, style, and context? Is the message calling forth the fruits of the Spirit or just righteousness?

Two people can speak the exact same words, but one operates as a prophet and the other does not. True prophets are aware that they are an instrument of God for delivering the message, and not its initiator. Mother Teresa loved to say, "I am like a little pencil in his hand."[1] Often true prophets begin with "The Lord says," because they are so convinced they are being used. How truly daring! I would feel presumptuous and unworthy to talk that way most of the time, yet prophets manage to combine such audacity with a posture of utter humility.

We must always ask, *Does the energy of the prophet point radically to the divine or stop with the pyrotechnics and oratory of the prophet himself?* We can see this in Elijah, who loves to call down fire from heaven and awe the crowd with what seems like a legitimate miracle, but this act ultimately leads to the creation of the angry, murderous mob that killed the prophets of Baal (1 Kings 18:38–40). Even apparent miracles must be discerned by their fruits.

Any opinion, liberal or conservative, might well be a good one, but what is its guiding energy and end point? Does it point beyond the messenger to the source and inspiration of the message itself? Does the speaker need to "win" too much? Are they driven by a need to be right? A true prophet leaves the success of the message in God's hands. Their job is to speak the truth and let go of the consequences or any need for an ideal response. Even if no one listens, they do not lose heart. That is a major indicator of the purity of their message.

JONAH: STUCK IN REWARD-PUNISHMENT

Jonah, another well-known Hebrew prophet, is also unfinished (even though I still love him). He rejects his divine commission at first, refusing to preach God's mercy to Nineveh, the capital of Assyria and Israel's ancient enemy. After he flees and boards a ship, he is cast overboard in a storm, swallowed by a great fish, and rescued in a marvelous manner. Only then does he obey God's call and go to Nineveh. The people repent upon hearing his message and thus are saved from God's wrath. But Jonah complains, angry because the Lord spared them. He is so detached from his own real message that he is disappointed when it succeeds!

From that point on, poor Jonah is simultaneously angry, lamenting, and praising Yahweh for four full chapters. His problem is that he cannot move beyond a dualistic reward-punishment worldview. Jonah thinks only Israel deserves mercy, whereas God extends total mercy to Jonah, to the pagan Ninevites who persecuted Jonah's people, and to those "who cannot tell their right hand from their left." To make the story complete, this mercy is even given to "all the animals" (Jonah 4:11)! The world of predictable good guys and always-bad guys collapses into God's unfathomable grace.

I love this story so much that I have collected images of a man in the belly of the whale for much of my adult life. I think I live in that whale's belly permanently, with loads of unresolved questions and painful paradoxes in my life. Yet God is always "vomiting" me up in the right place—in the complete opposite direction that I've been trying to run (Jonah 2:10).

The story of Jonah breaks all the expectations of who is right, and then remakes those expectations in favor of grace. It is a brilliant morality play, not a piece of dogmatic theology, as some try to make it. And yet it does have political implications, in the sense that it provokes us to change our notions of who deserves power and who doesn't.

Jonah thought he had the exclusive cachet of truth and thus could despise those to whom he was preaching. He wanted them to be wrong so that he could be right, yet in his anger at Nineveh and the Assyrian Empire, he failed to appreciate God's desire to offer even his enemies forgiveness and grace. In fact, he even resented their joining his "belief club." He struggled mightily to accept the new "political" arrangement.

When asked for a sign that he was the Messiah, Jesus said the sign of Jonah was the only one he was going to give (Matthew 12:39, Luke 11:29)! Really? What a provocation, and what a focusing! The Jonah story clearly says we are seeking both personal and social conversion—and Jesus later leans on this three-day journey of enlightenment as a metaphor for liminal space or transitioning. Jonah, who thinks that he and his religion are on top, is undone by "the pagans" in Nineveh. We call this a "power reversal story": a type often used in the Bible, from Joseph becoming Pharaoh's right-hand man to Job triumphing over his detractors. In every case, the protagonist must go "down" before he or she knows what "up" is, as Jesus himself famously models.

That's largely what makes it a "sign." As Jesus later points out, the Ninevites repent of their evil ways, while Israel did not (Matthew 12:41–42). The supposedly unconverted show themselves to be converted, while Jonah is shown to be unchanged, despite his three days in darkness.

We must not be discouraged, then, when people say, *You are making the message political and not spiritual!* The prophets speak about misuse of power, but always from an inspired basis, and at a higher level of morality. Think of Martin Luther King, Jr., and his crusade for civil rights; of Catherine of Siena's advocacy for reform of the clergy and peacemaking; of Sojourner Truth's activism for the abolition of slavery and civil rights for African Americans and women; of Cesar Chavez's work in organizing farmworkers. Their critiques and promises were stated in concrete historical terms, but with a clear spiritual meaning and motivation. Their messages were received gladly by the powerless and then exploited or rejected by prideful profiteers and narrow nationalists.

Unlike Jonah, a patriotic nationalist who wanted Nineveh to suffer, true prophets are always internationalists working to realize what Jesus will call the "kingdom of God." In their "political" advocacy, they point out and confront the power equations that are always corrupting human relations and the divine relationship, too. But it is not a partisan space that the prophets stand in. Look always for any overidentification with one particular side, group, or party. If someone is so identified with a side that they are unable to criticize or even see their own side objectively, the world will always be full of enemies, starting with the other competing candidate or the supporters of the opposite party. The thinking is always dualistic and largely about winning, not higher truth.

When we want to know if a prophet is mature, we can look for other qualities: Does the prophetic teacher need to be right, need badly to win the argument, or desire to humiliate the opposition? If so, the ego is likely running the show. What are their foundational sources? Current political correctness? Liberal or conservative agendas? Or prophets, saints, and mystic peacemakers? Jesus or John Wayne? What is the final goal of their moral or political position? Are they lost in rage, or do they have any space between themselves and their message? Are they overidentified with the truth or absoluteness of their own opinions? These are the concerns of a spiritually discerning person that help us sense and recognize the difference between a mere zealot and the much purer motivations and final goals of one who is doing God's work and not just their own.

THE CURIOUS CASE OF JOHN THE BAPTIZER

To conclude this discussion of unfinished prophets, let's look at one well-known case of a prophet who remained angry and verbally violent to the very end.

Although John the Baptizer has emerged as the archetypal image of a prophet for most Christians, I do not think he was a mature prophet. I say this for several important reasons. He surely was a humble and sincere man, quite ready to get out of the way for Jesus (Mark 1:7, Luke 3:16). His countercultural practices of wearing clothes of camel hair, subsisting on locusts and wild honey, and living in the wilderness certainly fit the profile of a prophet, and an admirable one at that. But John still had to get rid of his head before he could see from his heart. He enjoyed being a superior and judgmental outsider far too much. That's something we all must watch for in ourselves. The ego hides itself too well, and too easily, by making judgments. It's a good disguise. The judger always has a leg up on the judged, even if his judgment is wrong.

In the quote that opened this chapter, Jesus says that John is greater than anyone else and yet not great at all, because "the least is greater than he" by the new criteria of the kingdom of heaven (Matthew 11:11). That paradox is our definitive clue to seeing how John is unfinished. In the Gospels, he is portrayed as an ascetic and a firm moralist, preoccupied with purity and others' sins. He calls others a "brood of vipers" (Matthew 3:7), no better than rocks, and seems rather gleeful when he threatens them with "a fire that will never go out" (Matthew 3:12, JB). He stands at the gateway but has not yet heard Jesus's parables of the reign of God, or the teachings on meekness and poverty of spirit from the Sermon on the Mount. He does not yet know the language of healing, forgiveness, and grace that we find in Jesus and the mature prophets.

Thus, for me, John remains an unfinished prophet, operating not by lamentation, tears, or praise, but primarily by accusation—right up until his violent death. He publicly denounces Herod for marrying his niece, the wife of his late brother, and gets his head chopped off for his troubles (Matthew 14:3–12). This makes him a martyr, but only for a purity code and not for the new kingdom or indwelling spirit that Jesus proclaims. (For me, there is perhaps an archetypal meaning in the chopping off of John the Baptizer's head and presenting it on a platter! Like so many firebrands even today, he was trapped in his head. His martyrdom indeed made him a whole man, but by subtraction.)

Yet Jesus still honors John as a good and humble truthteller who points forward and beyond himself. When you are dealing with big truths, a little bit of inspiration goes a long way, as it does with the Baptizer. Even the legitimate and real reformer Martin Luther, an angry iconoclast in Catholic eyes, could be said to be more *conscious* and whole in his understanding of God's grace than most of the Catholic world at that time (albeit still angry and judgmental in many of his other pronouncements). Yet we do Scripture, and ourselves, a disservice if we take such unfinished prophets as examples to blindly follow, instead of recognizing their complexities and what they reveal about the much deeper role of God's love in human history. Lutheran friends in Germany told me they felt Martin Luther was a reformer more than a saint.

I sometimes wonder if the first two thousand years of Christianity have been more the religion of John the Baptizer than the interior, spiritual religion that Jesus brought into the world. Our ongoing feuds about the *who, when, where, how,* and *how much* of baptism, to name just one example, have caused lots of conflicts. The Anabaptists rejected infant baptism and insisted it could only be performed on those old enough to confess the faith. Catholics, meanwhile, have often insisted on rebaptism if the original baptism was not done by a Catholic priest. It is about group belonging for many of us more than real enlightenment.

The form of baptism has been just as important and controversial to Christians as circumcision was for the Jews (Galatians 6:15). When the foundational initiation rite is wrongly understood—seen as an identity badge and not an initiation into death itself (Romans 6:3–4)[2]—baptism became an entryway into a cult of innocence instead of a journey of solidarity with the wrong and the wronged.

I say all of this because I have seen so many Christians, on the one hand, and justice activists, on the other, who are morally correct in their actions but spiritually quite immature—doing the right things for the wrong reasons. (This was one of the major reasons I founded the Center for Action and Contemplation nearly forty years ago, and it is still true.) Some live a countercultural lifestyle, not really to help the poor, but to be seen as counterculturally chic. Many Catholics, meanwhile, assume we are saved by *doing church rules right* and not really by the pure grace and experienced love of God that radically rearranges our consciousness. Both groups are, in a sense, externally baptized with water, but not the "fire and Spirit" of Jesus's baptism.

Mature prophets make us conscious of both the patterns of grace and the endless disguises of ego. Thank God that he uses our mistakes to bring us to himself, so don't stop noticing your flaws and blind spots.

Traditionalists must know firmly that being obedient to divine and church law does not "save" them or prove their worthiness to God. Progressives must get out of their heads and move beyond the political correctness that passes for enlightenment. The divine love affair that characterizes the prophets is still mostly unknown to liberals or conservatives. Yet God still gifts both groups with their inherent goodness (really, God's goodness) and sets us all up to share this same wondrous gratuity with the rest of the world. This is the baptism of fire and the Holy Spirit that always characterizes a true and mature prophet.

JOB: EMBODYING THE FULL JOURNEY

Around the time I wrote this chapter, I was invited on a podcast to discuss a book I wrote many years ago on the story of Job.[3] It's unfortunate, I noted, that we categorize this book as wisdom literature, instead of listing Job among the prophets. As much as any person in Scripture, Job was acquainted with the tears of things. Elijah, Jonah, and John the Baptizer could only go so far, but Job embodies the transformed perspective of a mature prophet. (Islam seems to understand this, since Job appears as one of the twenty-five prophets named in the Koran.)[4]

All throughout his ordeal—the loss of his wealth, the death of his family, excruciating sicknesses that overtake his body—Job argues with God. He refuses to believe that God is punishing him; he also refuses to punish God, against the good advice of all his friends. Instead, he rebukes his four "religious" friends after they trot out all the classic arguments of retributive justice to lay guilt and shame on poor Job. He totally rejects—with all evidence to the contrary—any logic of divine retribution and reward. God is totally free because that is the nature of divine love. (God does not need to carry out our judgments.) We, created in the divine image, are therefore free from our own vengeance. And our neighbor is free from us. That is a safe universe.

You might say that Job begins, proceeds, and ends with self-correcting and self-absolving tears: "I am the man who obscured your designs with my empty-headed words. . . . I knew you then only by hearsay; but now, having seen you with my own eyes, I retract all I have said, and in dust and ashes I repent" (Job 42:3, 5–6, JB).

The book of Job is considered the conclusion, the summit, and the dead end of the Old Testament. It leaves God utterly free and mysterious, instead of presenting God as a punisher. If I had my way, I would ask people to read Job as a prophetic narrative, not a fairy tale of a patient man—and Job himself as a prophet as much as, if not more than, any of those listed. You could do far worse than allowing the prophets to lead you to the mind of Job.

I therefore ask you to read the rest of this book with these six premises in mind:

1. We have in great part created God in our own self-justifying image, just as Job's friends and the early-stage prophets tried to do.

2. The three monotheistic religions are still saddled with the image of a fearsome, capricious, and angry God. In practice, this misunderstanding wins out over every other narrative in Scripture, especially the central and important one of grace and mercy.

3. Religion is thus only in its early stages of transforming people and culture.

4. The prophets are indeed an early warning system against an angry picture of God, struggling with this entrapment themselves and overcoming it in many of their texts. The violence of God and religion must be directly and firmly undone inside the Bible itself, or it will only continue to undo all of us.

5. The transformative journey of the prophets from anger to tears to compassion is the journey of the God of the Bible and those who read the Bible with love.

6. Interestingly enough, the correlation between humanity's behavior and God's reward or punishment is the illusion that Job's dualistic friends insist on—and that Job rejects. Yet we find ourselves still largely on the side of the four mistaken friends to this day.

Remember this:

God does not love any of us because we are good.

God loves us because God is good.

God does not love Israel—or any group—because it is faithful and true. It never is!

God loves Israel because God is faithful and true, as God has been to both the church of Rome and to the church of Luther, Calvin, Knox, and every reformer since.

None of us is big enough (or shall I say small enough?) to hold all the implications of such an infinite love.

This is the new, everlasting, and unilateral covenant that the prophets themselves arrive at by trial and error. The steps to human maturity are always and necessarily immature. But if we stay with the process, we can witness both the infinite mystery and powerful mercy of God. We can join with Job in reciting his lasting creed:

> This I know: that my Redeemer lives
> And he, the Last, will take his stand on earth.
> He will awaken me and set me close to him,
> And from my flesh, I will look on God.
>   (Job 19:25–26)

I invite you to read the entire book of Job now as an argument for the new covenant and to see Job himself as the consummate prophet, although we have rarely, if ever, listed him as one.

God loves us because we are God's, not because we are right. Unconditional divine love is the fruit and result of this work of God in the soul. This clear conclusion, trust, and proclamation is the singular work of a mature and true prophet.

CHAPTER 7

The Alchemy of Tears: How We Learn Universal Sympathy and Grace

A re we the only animal that cries and sheds tears as an emotional response? It seems so, but what function do they serve for us? Jesus says we should be happy if we can weep, but why? Tears seem to appear in situations of sadness, happiness, awe, and fear—and usually come unbidden. What is their free message to us and to those who observe them? Has humanity gotten the message yet? Whatever it is, it is surely a message too deep for words.

There is only one book in the Bible named after an emotion: the book of Lamentations. Jeremiah is said to have written it as a way of expressing grief over the people's exile from Jerusalem when they were invaded by the Babylonians in 587 B.C. (We have already considered his other book, the one that bears his name, in depth in chapter 5.) But the book reads more like an expression of universal sadness over the human situation, or what is often called the "tragic sense of life." It's notable for an almost entire lack of anecdotes or clear examples. Elsewhere in the prophetic writings, we read references to specific rulers, kingdoms, and moments in history. Not here. This is universal sadness. It is an invitation to universal solidarity.

Saint Francis was depicted as crying all the time in his early biographies, and I always wondered why. I now believe, after fifty-four years of public ministry, that the gift of tears and the gift of healing are almost one and the same. "Blessed are those who weep," says Jesus, "for they will be comforted" (Matthew 5:4). Francis healed people and situations because he could deeply weep over them.

Jeremiah's sadness and tears of lamentation appear to be a divine evolution of anger. He was unable to sustain his rage at the people's collective foolishness and the felt injustice of everything—even his feelings that God had withdrawn himself instead of protecting his people from being captured: "Yahweh has spurned the bravest fighters I had. . . . And this is why I weep; my eyes dissolve in tears, since the comforter who could revive me is far away" (Lamentations 1:15–16, JB). In this way, the prophets, and Jeremiah in particular, invite us into a divine sadness about reality itself, much more than mere outrage at this or that event. The language then changes from anger at "sin" to pity over suffering and woundedness, yet still holds out for relief: "I will restore you to health and I will heal your wounds, says Yahweh" (Jeremiah 30:17a). Felt reality is invariably wept reality, and wept reality is soon compassion and kindness. Decisive and harsh judgments slip away in the tracks of tears.

When I look for examples of such evolution in our own

times, my mind recalls the Roman church's change in its official stance toward suicide. After Vatican II, the official emphasis shifted from punishment to empathy for the person and the
family. "Why further punish the victim and family?" the
Church concluded. I also think of Alcoholics Anonymous's
recognition that addiction is not a malicious moral failing but
"a sickness to be cured." I think of Pope Francis's willingness
to bless gay unions, which redefines the very notion of what a
blessing is. Anger can't make such switches. Tears can.

Has God changed, or have we just grown up enough to
hear a grown-up God? Old scripture passages of mercy and
pity that once seemed sentimental or impossible begin to finally make sense—and we suddenly notice their frequency, although they were always there. "You had left in tears, but I
brought you back. I guided you to springs of water by a
smooth path" (Jeremiah 31:9). This process of transformation
by way of tears is largely hidden and unconscious, characteris-
tic of the work of the Spirit.

My belief is that tears, although they look like a mere emo-
tive reaction, are much more: a deeply free action that many
do not enjoy. They proceed from deep inside, where we are
most truly ourselves. Tears reveal the depths at which and from
which we care.

COLLECTIVE SADNESS—AND REDEMPTION

Jeremiah's initial sadness is for the collective, represented by
the city of Jerusalem: "How lonely sits the city that once was
full of people!" he writes. "How like a widow she has become,
she that was great among the nations!" (Lamentations 1:1,
NRSV). This is the way that a mystic sees. Their tears are for

everything, and not just the momentary passing event. Although surely that, too.

Prophets deal in wholes and universals, and when they do assume specifics, they do so without dwelling on individual sentiment or outrage at shocking events. A good spiritual director can help you understand what Jesus said to the weeping women on the way to Calvary: "Do not weep for me, but for yourselves and your children" (Luke 23:28).

This is an attitude of grief over universal and ontological evil, which is very different from our modern-day fixation on sensational anecdotes. *Life is inherently sad,* the prophets want us to know. *Humanity is foundationally unfaithful to love and truth,* they seem to shout. In this way, prophets act more as philosophers than as journalists or pundits, inviting us into the divine pity for all of creation. This is major and central if we hope to understand the heart of Jeremiah, the four "servant songs" of Isaiah, and most especially Jesus's message from the cross.

Most folks invariably apologize for or try to hide their tears. One wonders why. Do they not want the deep self to be revealed? Perhaps it is because tears are so inexplicable? So out of control? Operating by their own rules? Humiliating? Always! Tears invite participation in a wider world and pull us out of our isolation.

When we cry, we are revealing our truest, most loving self. We seem to be afraid to trust, much less show, this secret side of ourselves. Yet it's there in each of us. Whenever I witness any scene of personal reconnection of lost family members, or even people reunited with their long-lost dogs, I sob. When I do, I usually feel ashamed and try to hide it. I do not think I personally have any deep loss or abandonment issues, but I sob like a baby nevertheless.

When I led male initiation rites for ten years here at Ghost Ranch in New Mexico, we took guests through a shortened five-day process for modern men. After two days of invitation into liminal space and facing our own death, we talked about grief and sadness. It was on this third day, the "day of grief," that most men made their breakthrough—or didn't. Some could not access their tears, but most would at least begin to talk about their hidden sadness, which changed the entire character and freedom of their grief. They all felt sadness, but few had a name for it or the courage to cry over it in a group.

I also think of two Maasai warriors I met in Kenya years ago. They were given permission by their elders to show me their "caves of grief," where, as part of their initiation journey, they had to learn to literally cry for all the world—plants, animals, fellow humans, earth itself—before they could continue on to manhood. Imagine! Would that we had such a ritual journey for American politicians, businesspeople, prisoners, soldiers, and clergy.

In my experience, tears have helped me glimpse the big secret that I still only half know—that human beings are really made of love and for love. *And we still don't know it!* We can only cry it. Until a divine form of compassion enters the scene (and this might be the naked narrative underlying the whole Bible), we do not enjoy the deep alchemy that morphs human rage and judgment into holy sadness.

At the exact midpoint of Lamentations (3:21–26), Jeremiah brings his sad symphony and requiem Mass to a climax—returning suddenly to an ever-faithful love that allows him to "recover hope": "But this I call to mind . . . his mercies never come to an end; they are new every morning; great is thy faithfulness" (Lamentations 3:21–23, NRSV). Anger keeps us trapped both in ourselves and outside ourselves. We need to be broken out of it and connected with its underlying source, which is often our and everyone else's pain. Tears can do that. As therapists and researchers now teach, trauma (along with its resultant anger or depression) mostly resides at the cellular level, in the body more than the mind. This is why the responses of the mind and talk therapy, even if accurate, often fall short in healing a traumatized person.

Note how in the Gospels Jesus almost always touches people when he heals them. It is the body itself that holds our fear, our anger, and our debilitating memory. It is the body that must somehow *be held and healed and spoken to.* The text goes out of its way to say so, as in Luke 5:14: "Jesus reached out and touched the leper, saying 'Of course I want to heal you.'" Or when he takes the seemingly dead girl by the hand and says, "Get up" in Mark 5:42.

We all need to feel and know, at this cellular level, that we are not the first ones who have suffered, nor will we be the last. Instead, we are in *one universal parade*—God's "triumphal procession," as Paul calls it (2 Corinthians 2:14, NRSV), using the metaphor of a Roman triumph after a great victory. In this parade, he says, we are all "partners" (2 Corinthians 2:14, JB) with both the living and the dead, walking alongside countless ancestors and descendants who were wounded and longed for healing. This idea, "the communion of saints," became the last phrase added to the Apostles' Creed centuries later, almost as if it took us a while to recognize its importance. Someday, maybe we will have the courage to add "the communion of sinners," too.

The body of Christ is one great and shared sadness and one continuous joy, and we are saved just by remaining connected to it. This is partly what the French anthropologist Lucien Lévy-Bruhl meant by his term *participation mystique,* describing how material events can be seen as reflecting deeper truths about reality. *Participation* names something very real and concrete about how all of us humans are connected to one another as an invisible collective. And how we experience healing!

Since the Enlightenment, however, we have been trained to believe that we each can "do it my way," like Frank Sinatra, instead of participating in everybody else's great parade. As I often say, *if we do not mythologize our pain, all we can do is pathologize it.* My editors invariably compliment me when I frame my point well and criticize me when I so often fail to do so. You would think I would have gotten this advice by now. In the same way, we Westerners have lost the ability to frame the significance of our own little lives. We no longer believe or live as if we are an inherent part of a much bigger story. I suspect that "pagans" who grew up with the myths of Ulysses and Athena or the Corn Mothers or Kali more easily found meaning and consolation for their pain than we do today. We are not a part of the cosmic dance that created Greek comedy and tragedy and led the Pueblos of the Southwest to dance and carve kachinas as a way of marking human events or emotions. Helping people see that they are cooperating members of a performance that is already showing—and will keep showing—is surely why so many of the religions of Indigenous people were, at their heart, ancestor worship.

This participation in others' sadness is precisely what should happen when we gaze upon the crucified one, upon a child bleeding alone on the streets of Gaza, or upon any act of human tragedy. As Zechariah 12:10–12 says: "When they look upon one they have pierced, they shall mourn for him, as one mourns for an only child, and weep bitterly over him" (also see John 19:37). Somehow this empathy liberates us, even as it scours the soul. That is what Christians really mean when they say they are "saved" by the cross. Being present in such a way can make all of our suffering one and even divine, for those who gaze upon it regularly and with reverence—like a sacrament.

You don't think yourself into crying. You cry *yourself,* if you will allow, into daring new ways of thinking and feeling. Because tears are a form of allowing more than a willing, they lend themselves much more easily to the language of spirit.

The saints and mystics who wept before the cross were first of all weeping universal tears for the suffering world. All of reality is "signed" with the cross, and our tears often become a slow, sad recognition that we also are now on the same tragic, but also victorious, path. All things first and finally deserve tears much more than hatred, fixing, or denial.

If we are not saved together, and in spite of our worst selves, I do not know how we are saved at all. Perhaps this is why the nuns I knew in childhood told us daily to "offer up" our little sufferings for "the poor souls in purgatory." How much those nuns trusted and taught our childlike faith! I don't know if I helped any poor souls praying for John or Mary who had died, but it sure helped me—and almost immediately. Lévy-Bruhl's *participation mystique* again!

COSMIC SUFFERING AND COSMIC HOPE

I encourage you to read the entire text of Lamentations (only five short chapters) the next time you are seriously suffering from grief or sadness. Lamentations has been called the "tabula rasa prayer" because it has the power to let you project your own sadness onto this universal text and thus find healing in participation with the millions who have found similar solace there: "She passes her nights weeping, the tears run down her cheeks. Not one of all her lovers remains to comfort her, her friends have all betrayed her and become her enemies" (Lamentations 1:2, JB).

You can recognize in such an invitation, *I am not the first nor the last to feel this dying. I can now choose to be a weak but willing member of the whole communion of saints!* Surely such solidarity is our salvation, rather than private purity or personal wholeness. Paul called it living "en Cristo," a phrase that he used hundreds of times to name the shape and coherence of our collective participation mystique.

Maybe hope needs to be cosmic hope to be hope at all. Maybe pain needs to be borne together, and for all time; it is very hard to bear alone, or in the moment. We fight it as unfair and undeserved when we could instead carry it as an act of human and loving solidarity.

I often think that Christianity, or any religion for that matter, would be much more effective as a constant choice for human solidarity instead of this useless "cult of innocence" that it became. Simone Weil, the French mystic and resistance leader, spent her whole life seeking radical solidarity with human suffering, as did Saint Albert Chmielowski of Poland, a lesser-known figure who was orphaned at an early age and had his leg amputated without anesthesia. He went on to take up shelter with the poor with whom he was working in Krakow, and founded a whole brotherhood to do the same. I would call both of them prophets and harbingers of a much-needed future Christianity. If you have not heard of either of them, it is perhaps because we do not tend to admire, or even recognize, deep identification and quiet solidarity as much as we idealize heroic martyrdom. This collective consciousness is the femi-

nine way of Mary standing at the foot of the cross, comple-
menting Jesus's agonizing death with her own weeping and
public vulnerability. Here is that feminine performative prophecy again. Why do we only admire one form of love?

The three universal spiritual practices of almsgiving, fasting,
and prayer are ways of seeking such union. They are best seen
as acts of loving solidarity with another person or group—and
not really attempts to talk God into doing something about it.
In my charismatic days, we often spoke of "the gift of tears,"
as did many of the saints. It was a kind of crying for *everything*
occasioned by the tragedy of *any one thing*. And it so often
preceded and accompanied the other, more impressive spiritual gifts, like healing, anointed preaching, prophetic speech,
and praying in tongues.

We seem to have forgotten this connection. Healing work
in the hospital, for example, has long been considered heroic
(and it is), but it has taken us a long time to recognize the
importance of bereavement ministries, hospice care, and grief
counseling. Ministries of mere presence are seen as optional,
even superfluous. It is our classic preference of the masculine
over the feminine: doctors over nurses, priests over nuns, the
immediate over the arduous. "Don't just stand there, do
something" feels intuitively right to most of us.

In Lamentations, such grief is not passive, and sadness does
not have the final word. The desire to move beyond grief happens, but only in the final four verses: "Make us come back to
you, Yahweh, and we will come back. Renew us as in days of
old" (Lamentations 5:21). The act of lamentation has finally
softened the writer's heart to compassion and prayer. All true
prophets, like Ezekiel, eat of the scroll of "lamentations, weeping, and woe," and only in time does it become "sweet as
honey" (Ezekiel 2:10, 3:3, JB) because of its enlightening ef-

fects. That is the slow alchemy I observe in almost all of the prophets.

Lamentations ends with a final warning against "an anger that knows no limit" (5:22, JB), which too often we have confused for God's anger. But this surely must refer to our own anger and our own spirit and expectation of rejection. If we believe that God is angry in the way that humans are, then it is too easy for all of us to end up being angry "without limit." In fact, if we believe the Creator is always critiquing, judging, and punishing everything, it should be no surprise that our entire universe is bathed in rage and resentment. Isn't this, in fact, much of our world today? Someone must show us the way through. It cannot be done by law or order, but with a remembering of the great and divine pity modeled and taught by saints and prophets.

I surely believe some form of projection of our anger onto others is at the heart of the nonstop world wars of the "Christian" nations. It's at the center of those cultures that encourage punitive or emotionally withholding parents or people with "stiff upper lips." Crying, at its best, teaches us to hold the emotion instead of projecting it elsewhere.

In the prophecies of Jeremiah, all hopes for the future of the Jewish people lie in those who endured a three-stage process of transformation: first, those who entered into exile; second, those who retained hope and did not turn bitter in and during that exile; and, third, those who returned from exile with generativity and praise in their hearts instead of self-pity.

These people are the change agents for culture, paralleling the classic three stages of purgation, illumination, and union. Each of these stages operates as a change agent in different ways. *Into, through, and back home* could well be the necessary movements for any of us. Most of our effort and egoic training has been an effort to avoid, deny, and turn around any unfortunate setbacks. Jeremiah could be called the prophet of the whole journey: into purgation, through illumination, and finally resting in union.

HEAVEN ALL THE WAY TO HEAVEN

We use many different words to describe major human change and growth: *transformation, awakening, enlightenment, conversion,* or simply *evolving awareness.* Just as life, by its very nature, never stays the same, we cannot stay the same, either. It is not about marching doggedly in one direction—as many believers have been unfairly taught. Nor is it about order, and more ordering, and return to ordering, as my early Catholic schooling and seminary taught me. The psychologist and theologian Gerald May put it well when he said that kind of dogged determination only made us terribly "willful" but not gracefully "willing," which is where growth in virtue lies.[1] Virtue is more like a chemical change in a petri dish than the well-considered lines of an engineer's diagram.

Carl Jung, after many years of studying people who grew and those who didn't, came to several unique and helpful constructs to describe the phenomenon of human flourishing. I will only present a few here, but to start with, he says that humans are driven toward an archetypal energy of *wholeness,* which most of us cannot define precisely.[2] Some call it happiness, some salvation, some maturity, some evolution, but most folks sense intuitively that life is moving them somewhere, often without their full or conscious approval. To have no sense of such movement is what it must mean to be in hell—or at least purgatory—figuratively speaking. All spiritual growth, on the other hand, somehow implies that heaven can accumulate in us, and we are already going there. As Dorothy Day wrote, "It's heaven all the way to heaven."[3] What a mistake to put it off until later, although that has been a crucial consolation for many with very hard lives.

Jung describes this movement toward wholeness as primarily energized and facilitated by conflicts of many different kinds. (I used to use the word *suffering* in most of my books, but *conflicts* might here describe the experience better.) Conflicts always have a character of paradox to them:

desire versus rejection of it

attraction versus fear of things

male versus female

right versus wrong

unity versus autonomy

me versus not me

life versus death

Christian versus non-Christian

Republican versus Democrat

On and on such conflicts go, in every realm of our lives. Our temptation is, of course, to choose one side and discount or eliminate the other one. Such thinking is rightly called "dualistic."[4] Either-or choices seem much easier and simpler in the short run, which is where most of us live, but they are not that helpful in the long run. You only realize that is true over time, which is why almost all traditional cultures admired age and not youth.

We like efficiency and ease more than just about anything else. But don't be fooled! To operate with this dualistic mind, you have to split your cognition in two—and thus reduce its power by half! We all pay a huge price in this trade-off, because there is always a third, fourth, or fifth insight or solution to uncover, but it does not seem to be worth the trouble when we can fall back on one of our two usual and easy choices.

We move toward wholeness, I am convinced, by holding these conflicts and paradoxes together in the soul—more than the mind—and letting them work their natural chemistry there. It is all about waiting trustfully, holding without panicking, and anticipating, even in the silence, that an answer will be given. It is hope added to faith and love. Those who trust this process create a new future while others just repeat the past over and over. Time and further experience are the leaven. Somehow we must present ourselves as a willing container to hold all of our conflictual paradoxes together in a temporary and hopefully creative tension until we can experience a bigger and always more compassionate self.

If we can hold those paradoxes with a certain love, an even deeper love will show itself once you stop fighting it or denying its ubiquitous presence. It builds up with use! Jeremiah says that anyone who teaches otherwise is a false prophet: "And you must not listen to him. He is a mere diviner, dreamer, soothsayer, or sorcerer who tells you *not* to be subjects of the king of Babylon!" (Jeremiah 27:9–10).

Following his leading, I say, as it were, that you must go into Babylon (exile), and find a new kind of freedom there. Don't believe those who tell you that you can grow while staying in full control. It is a lie. *In all of our lives, deeper love has to do with giving up some measure of control.* Jeremiah advises a giving up of control to a larger loving force. He even lets himself be a living pantomime of this state, living for some period with a rope and noose around his neck (Jeremiah 27:2). As all authentic initiation rites teach, you must die before you die— and then you will not be afraid of dying. Giving up control assumes there is someone to give control up to—someone I can trust to do an even better job.

I shared earlier, but love to repeat, the final words of the Buddhist Heart Sutra, "*Gate, gate, paragate, parasamgate,*" which means "Gone, gone, utterly gone, all has gone over to the other shore." There's been so much *gate* in the last ten years of my life that I cannot become overreliant on anything self-affirming or self-validating. I can't help but see the shadow side of everything now. I have to watch the cynicism, but on my better days I'm not angry about it; I'm just sad about it, like I say in this book. And this is a sadness I can live with, a sadness I can love with. Things do not have to be perfect for me to reverence them, respect them, honor them, love them, and forgive them.

ALCHEMY: THE PROCESS OF WHOLE-MAKING

In describing the growth process, Carl Jung uses the brilliant metaphor of alchemy. Alchemy was an early, prescientific form of chemistry by which people sought to create gold by mixing the right elements, for the right amount of time, to the right degree, and at the right temperature. While the practical results of alchemy were mixed, to put it mildly, Jung nonetheless applies it as a helpful metaphor for human transformation.

That is how I also am using it. He describes at least seven central alchemical phenomena that most of us experience as life does its work on us:

conjunctio: the combining of contrary ingredients

solutio: a loss of one substance to create a new admixture

sublimatio: refining lesser ingredients into higher ones

coagulatio: turning something ephemeral into something concrete

calcinatio: the hardening needed to coalesce into substance

mortificatio: necessary dying for movement between stages

putrefactio: changing even to the point of appearing unattractive

These seven stages of alchemy are all spontaneous inner reactions to outer or conflicting events. They are profoundly psychological—and in my opinion, deeply theological, too. The secret is to hold the different ingredients together without seeking an answer, a goal, an outcome, a product, or a judgment. Let them all marinate together for as long as it takes to get to a free, accepting *yes.* You can see why the mystery and transformation of alchemy would appeal to a depth psychologist. In his lifetime of study, Jung found it to be the ideal metaphor for what a good therapist or spiritual guide does.[5]

I don't know that a spiritual director can operate well without intuitively understanding such alchemy. Without it, we tend to expect law to achieve the purposes of Spirit. We expect self-help programs to lead us beyond the self. It does not work. And the irony is that both Jesus (in the Sermon on the Mount) and Paul (in Romans 3 and Galatians 3–5) already taught this quite passionately. I think of Paul's bold claim: "The Law served to guard us until Christ came and we could move into trust. Now that this new trust level has shown itself, we no longer need the old guardian" (Galatians 3:24–25). Wow, how dangerous is that? Most of us prefer the immediately measurable—and Spirit is never that. *Wait and pray*, a good spiritual director will say. *Do not do, but allow and trust and wait, as Jesus advised his disciples in the garden of Gethsemane.*

In Jung's eyes, the alchemists' search for gold was a search for human wholeness, but falsely projected onto the outer world of a precious metal. He ends up sounding like a Christian, Islamic, or Buddhist mystic when he describes human selfhood as the ground that remains once you have withdrawn all your idealized projections from money, sex, power, and other people, and learn to live out of your naked identity in God: for which he used the word *Self*, with a capital *S*.

The real genius of Jung's metaphor is that it describes a rather spontaneous, organic, natural movement. Our only job is to keep the ego from trying to control everything, which it loves to do. Egocentricity keeps us small and self-centered, with no interest in anything beyond ourselves.

Jung's process of growth sounds a lot like religious faith at its more mature level. It is also similar to the Chinese Taoists' understanding of *wu wei:* the notion that "doing nothing" can be an admirable form of trust, or effortless action. You let *it* be (whatever *it* is), and time can and will do its own work of growth, admixture, and integration. It is a very different agenda from the one we normally practice. As Moses told the

Israelites at the edge of the Red Sea, "You have to do nothing but to keep still. Yahweh will do the fighting for you" (Exodus 14:14). Just when they were ready to start running!

A quiet allowing is much to be preferred to any strict controlling. Yet this is quite amazing and totally counterintuitive for most of us. As Isaiah says:

> Who ever heard of such a thing?
> Who ever saw anything like this?
> Is a country born in one day?
> Is a nation brought forth all at once?
> That Zion, not yet in labor,
> Should bring forth children. (Isaiah 66:8)

Prophetic *wu wei,* you might say.

THE PROPHETIC ARC

I began this book by saying that I saw in the prophets a slow but real movement from extended rage and anger (where many of us tire of them), through different forms of holy disorder, to tears and sadness, and then morphing into compassion as their mature response to evil and injustice. Very commonly their sadness (as in Lamentations) is interrupted by bursts of praise, a pattern we also see in many of the Psalms. I am convinced that with this simple code and pattern, you have the central key for reading the prophets fruitfully.

Let's end this chapter with one classic example of lamentation breaking into praise. It's called the "canticle of Hezekiah," and we find it in the third part of Isaiah (chapter 38), after the exile in Babylon. For me, it hauntingly describes the

deep contentment of a king being promised fifteen more years
of life after being readied to face a painful death:

> From dawn to night, you surround me,
> I cry aloud till the morning, like a lion you have
>   crushed all my bones. . . .
> I am twittering like a swallow or a crane, moaning
>   like a dove. . . .
>
> Lord, my heart will live for you,
> my spirit will live for you alone.
> You will cure me and give me life,
> my suffering will turn to health.
>
> It is you who have kept my soul
> from the pit of nothingness,
> you have thrust all my sins
> behind your back.
>
> For Sheol does not praise you,
> Death does not extol you. . . .
>
> The living, the living are the ones who praise you,
> as I do today. (Isaiah 38:12–14, 16–19)

Our divinely inspired transformation is a nonstop, subtle,
autonomous action that we now call grace. It is not a substance or a thing that can be quantified, but a metamorphosis
in the soul, a profound change of our inner processor, a new
consciousness, an utterly changed motivation, a reversing of
our engine without our seeming consent. But our *yes* is important and necessary. When I was in seventh grade, an elderly

Irish nun, Sister Clara, would tell us almost daily, with great emphasis, "You must cooperate with grace." I wonder if we could even talk that way anymore?

Grace is never induced by morality or piety or even law. It comes like the best and worst of our tears: usually uninvited, uncreated, unchosen, and unexpected, a pure creation out of nothing. From there, tears do their work, if we will just allow a little secret chemistry in the soul. Such subtle *solutio* is already and always at work.

CHAPTER 8

The Three Isaiahs:
The Heart of Prophecy

For many of us, the name Isaiah is synonymous with the word *prophet,* and rightly so. He is quoted the most often in the New Testament and in the liturgies for major Christian feast days and seems to have been the most influential in shaping both Judaism and Christianity. Since the quotes we hear are usually poetic and positive, we probably picture a nice old bearded grandpappy prophesying in the city square and given to rage only when appropriate. But there is so much more to this important book of the Old Testament, and what it reveals about the prophets' path from anger to sadness to praise.

Biblical scholars of the past century have suspected that the book of Isaiah is the work of at least three writers, not one, and was produced over a period that included both the exile and the return from Babylon. What has come to be known as the "III Isaiah theory" provides a perfect example of how knowing the historical context is necessary to understanding the text. Such a view of Scripture helps us realize that real people in real contexts wrote the Bible; it did not fall out of thin air onto an inspired page. When we take Scripture literally and uncritically, without a bit of study, we can make it say whatever we want, even if it is the justification of war, slavery, fabulous private wealth, gun culture, polygamy, or genocide—all of which has been done without shame by people who read the Bible literally.

Using what is known as the "historical-critical method" of biblical interpretation gives us much more honesty and accountability in our interpretations, as well as new insights that archeology, anthropology, and psychology now offer us. Most mainline churches assume that some form of historical-critical methodology is the most helpful way to understand the Bible and—even more important—to tap into its real power to convict, convert, and change individuals and every culture's idolatries. Rather than reading the Bible inside our own bubble, we must allow the Bible to read us.

I ISAIAH

I Isaiah (chapters 1–39) was written by the prophet Isaiah, who lived, preached, and prophesied after his call around 742 B.C. (another time of war with Assyria), well before the exile into Babylon (597–538 B.C.). He sets the lasting style and pattern, which is the movement from anger at social injustices, to lamentation over them in chapters 13 to 23, even including laments for Israel's enemies: And so for Moab "my whole

being quivers like lyre strings" (Isaiah 16:11, JB). Here we
begin to see the evolution of love culture in its expansion from
self-love, to neighbor love, to love of otherness, which is the
very nature of God's love.

We might say that this amazing quote (along with the many
others like it) exemplifies early "third-way thinking," in which
the tragic side of other people's reality and the pain of the
world *are suffered and held and allowed to change Isaiah and
his readers more deeply.* This thinking represents a monumental
advance in consciousness. Religious motivation is no longer
based on fear of punishment but on compassion for *all*
suffering—not just mine or ours. It makes way for God's universal compassion to eventually emerge for each of the three
Isaiahs. One can safely say that, because of prophetic speech,
the Jewish religion is about a gradual purification not just of
action but also of motive and intention. To "do something for
God" is another way of saying to do it for the common good.
It becomes an exponential track of growth.

I Isaiah's experience was expressed in the classic praise
"Holy, holy, holy" (Isaiah 6:3), which mystics and liturgies still
use in the presence of ultimate transcendence. We might now
translate it as "Awesome, awesome, awesome" or even "Beyond, beyond, beyond." I Isaiah's call and inaugural vision in
chapter 6:1–13 are classic and profound. The only trouble
with such an awesome sense of divine transcendence is that it
makes the gap so huge between God and humanity that it is
hard to overcome. Left to itself, it usually creates a religion of
purity and impurity more than a religion of love. But not here.
At the beginning, Isaiah says, "What a state I am in. I am lost.
I am a man of unclean lips" (Isaiah 6:5). In the presence of
total gracious beyondness, his human ego is both undone and
utterly redone at the same time! This is reorder enlighten-

ment, offered right at the very beginning of his journey. There is no mention of working up to it at all.

But in the meantime, Isaiah still has a lot of angry oracles against foreign and domestic enemies to work through before he can experience a cosmic sadness in chapter 24 and eventually express liberating praise in chapter 33. He gets the full quantum packet of awesomeness in one inaugural vision, and then takes the rest of his life to unpack what it means (as is true for many of us). Rationalists cannot easily allow this kind of unitive knowing. Prophets such as Isaiah are like William Blake, the English mystic and poet, who wrote in "Auguries of Innocence":

> To see a World in a Grain of Sand
> And a Heaven in a Wild Flower
> Hold Infinity in the palm of your hand,
> And Eternity in an hour.[1]

Even the name of this poem seems to imply an ideal imagining of an unwounded state (*innocens* meaning "unwounded") that I am calling reorder. We think it's about returning to an original, unsullied state, when in reality the prophetic way is to pass through disorder to a new stage that does not eliminate or deny the tears of things but instead includes them at a new level. Divine perfection is precisely the ability to include imperfection! God forgives by including the mistake and letting go of the need to punish it. We can do the same.

We also must trust that what seems like disorder is the portal through which we move from what we think is lasting order to something genuinely new. We must include the shadow side in the solution. Forgiveness is not denial, but "yes and": Yes, you did wrong, *and* I forgive you. It happens by grace over time, as we see in every one of the true prophets. "You must listen and listen again, and not understand, see and see again but not perceive . . . until you understand with your heart and are healed by me," Yahweh says to Isaiah (Isaiah 6:9–10).

Matthew even repeats this in his gospel, where Jesus explains the meaning of his parable of the sower (13:14–15). This is Jesus's language of growth and staging.

Gradualism is the only honest way one can know spiritual things without becoming ego-inflated. How different religion would have been for history if we had known not just with our minds but with this kind of patient searching and humble waiting.

Maybe this language will help. Our first perception of reality is always child's play constructed around ourselves and our limited world, and we are necessarily at its center. Something must deconstruct this performative megalomania, if you will allow me. Love and suffering are its two major wrecking balls, the first being positive and the second seemingly negative. The prophets teach us how to let both love and suffering operate together. This is their unique method and the only real way our personal redemption can also lead to a restoration of our surrounding culture. The second Isaiah also demonstrates this brilliantly.

II ISAIAH

"But Zion said, 'The Lord has forsaken me, my Lord has forgotten me.' Does a woman forget her baby at the breast? Or fail to cherish the son of her womb? Yet even if these forget, I will never forget you" (Isaiah 49:14–15). These words of trust, from the second Isaiah, are remarkable. Despite writing before the end of the exile in Babylon, around 597–538 B.C., this author already trusts that God will rescue the people of Israel. His or her ego construction is already positive and relational (the mother's gaze), so a wrecking ball for the ego is hardly needed. All this author has to do is de-center all of the superiority notions of their nationhood, ethnicity, and culture, which the exile unfortunately achieves. As the Israelites found in Babylon, through three generations of humiliation, the only shadow more hidden than our own is the agreed-on shadow of our group, where our tendencies toward violence and persecution are so commonly reinforced. The Israelites were perhaps shown this lesson by seeing the Babylonians enacting their group superiority during the exile, but they persisted in holding on to their own group shadow as well. A hard lesson to learn indeed!

Do you see the classic progression? First, order, in the Jewish history of Exodus and the journey into the Promised Land; second, holy disorder, through the exile in Babylon; and third, reorder, a rebuilding on a new foundation, which now includes the wisdom of both previous stages, where they now regulate and balance one another. Each group or generation thinks it has the final and full answer, until the next major social movement or next philosophical genius comes along, or the Webb telescope discovers new boundaries.

It is never just a straight line of better explanation and enforcement of the first order. That is a common assumption, especially for conservatives, while liberals tend to think of ever-better ways to reveal and pursue disorder. This won't work, either, as we can see in our own time.

Chapters 40–55 of Isaiah are also known as the "book of consolation." There is a conspicuous lack of militaristic, win-lose language in II Isaiah despite the suffering of exile. A different kind of victory is being sought on a new interior level. This, too, expresses an evolution of consciousness and motivation. It changes everything and moves us into what we will call the new covenant in Jeremiah. II Isaiah senses what is coming—a religion based on grace and not on supposed perfection or performance: "Shout for joy, you barren women who bore no children! Break into shouts of joy and gladness, you who were never in labor! For the sons of the forsaken one are more in number than the sons of the wedded wife" (Isaiah 54:1, JB).

For me, II Isaiah is the epitome of awakened reorder prophecy. The four famous "servant songs" (42:1–9, 49:1–6, 50:4–11, 52:13–53:12) are a clear turning point in the whole Bible—the expectation of a very different kind of liberator and a very different kind of liberation: "The Lord Yahweh comes to my help, so that I am untouched by those who insult me. I set my face like flint, I know I shall not be put to shame" (Isaiah 50:7). These are not songs that the masculine psyche can easily appreciate. All four are almost entirely in the language of vulnerability and powerlessness, which Jesus fully enacted, but we are still and probably always will be unprepared for:

> Here is the one I uphold,
> my chosen one in whom my soul delights.
> I have given him my spirit
> that he may bring true justice to the nations.
> He does not cry out or shout aloud,
> or make his voice heard in the streets. . . .
>
> From the beginning I have been silent,
> I have kept quiet, held myself in check.
> I groan like a woman in labor,
> I suffocate, I stifle. (Isaiah 42:1–2, 14)

II Isaiah is written in the highly evolved language of the nonviolent resister whom we only began to hear by the twentieth century, in prophets like Mahatma Gandhi, Rosa Parks, Bayard Rustin, Simone Weil, and Dorothy Day. It is the language of redemptive suffering instead of the universally admired language of redemptive violence. It is "one octave too high,"[2] as the rabbi Abraham Joshua Heschel says, compared with our preferred can-do, problem-solving, fixing mind.

I cannot say it strongly enough. This is an utterly new tactic and a new agenda, and hardly a "tactic" at all.

III ISAIAH

When you read the four "servant songs" prayerfully, they lead directly to the incipient universalism we will find in what we will now call III Isaiah: a grief-filled message that ultimately results in praise.

III Isaiah is the prophet Jesus quotes directly when he first introduces himself in the synagogue in Nazareth:

> The Spirit of God has been given to me,
> Yahweh has anointed me.
> He has sent me to bring good news to the poor,
> To bind up hearts that are broken,
> To proclaim liberty to captives,
> Freedom to those in prison,
> To proclaim the Year of Favor from the Lord.*
> (Luke 4:18–19, quoting Isaiah 61:1–2)

---

* The "jubilee year," when all debts are forgiven (Leviticus 25:10–11).

Jesus, like the prophet he quotes, reveals not only his self-confidence but also his likely and intended audience. His message of good news is not likely to be sought after or heard by the comfortable and the secure, he seems to say, but by the poor, the captives, the blind, and the oppressed—which fully explains Jesus's behavior throughout the rest of his ministry.

Neither Jesus nor the suffering servant sought failure for its own sake, but they did seek what such a perspective uniquely teaches: that *the rejected and silenced ones always expose what the culture actually idealizes.* Our attitude of near loathing toward the homeless and those on welfare, for example, shows that we overly idealize material success in the United States. The prophets have a way of recognizing victim blame and scapegoating long before the rest of us—anticipating the later Christian desire to honor the image of God in all people. I hope we can now enjoy both revelations: nonviolent philosophies and an entirely unitive theology giving objective dignity to all.

Notice that Jesus deliberately does not quote the final line of the full, yet contradictory, Isaiah passage: "to proclaim a day of vengeance from our God." Instead, he "rolled up the scroll, gave it back to the attendant and sat down" (Luke 4:19–20). The three staccato breaks are rather undeniable and telling visuals: "rolled up," "gave it back," and "sat down." It's almost as though Jesus is tired of making God into one who limits and threatens, instead of the limitless one whom the passage has just talked about, and so different from the glorious vision of the New Jerusalem Isaiah has just described in the whole of chapter 60.

Jesus refuses to let Isaiah end with caution and fear. Fortunately, we see that Isaiah does not stay there, either. Later in the book, he exclaims:

> I am ready to be approached by those who do not
>   consult me,
> Ready to be found by those who do not seek me.
>   I say,
> "I am here. I am here!" by a nation that does not
>   even invoke my name. (Isaiah 65:1)

This sounds like so much availability and generosity from God's side, perhaps too much for us to hope for. And yet this is where III Isaiah lands for the rest of the prophecy, until the very final verse, 66:24, where he covers his bases with a seeming allusion to the fires of Gehenna. (They had God-stingy inquisitors in his day, too, I guess.)

That final, punitive verse evolved over time in our religious imagination into the literal description of the unquenchable fire of Gehenna, and thus hell. But in Jewish teaching, Sheol and Hades have no connotations of punishment, and certainly not eternal punishment. The metaphor of fire in the whole Bible is almost entirely a "refiner's fire" of purification in this world, not a fire of torture in the next. (Except perhaps for Matthew, who seems to like throwing in a negative threat at the end of many of his parables. See Matthew 13:30, 42, 50.) What damage this has done to the hearing and trusting of the entire gospel message! You cannot follow, much less imitate, a God who revels in eternal punishments from the get-go. That makes God far too dangerous and ogre-like to work with, particularly if we hope to move toward any goal of loving union with God. If only the prophets could correct this misapprehension in our own time.

Most scholars now think that III Isaiah (chapters 55–66) was written by a whole school of Isaiah-style prophets who emerged after the exile around 538 B.C., all using the name

Isaiah because it had come to have such authority. The apocalyptic style we find in these chapters reflects the Israelites' recovery from the historical trauma of the exile and helps them comprehend how such a total catastrophe could happen to the chosen people of God. (Maybe this also explains the inexplicable final verse in chapter 66?) *Utter failure could happen again, but now we have strong evidence that it won't,* would be my interpretation of that macabre final verse.

Still, the final chapters of III Isaiah entertain themes of universal liberation and salvation for all, beginning with eunuchs and foreigners (56:1–7), along with agnostics and the barely interested (65:1–9), continuing with many hints of universal salvation (through most of chapter 65), and moving into a total cosmology with a "new heavens and a new earth" (65:17; see also 66:22). These images will return again at the end of the New Testament (Revelation 21:1). Thank God the Bible ends with an optimistic hope and vision, instead of an eternal threat that puts the whole message off balance and outside of love.

THE CLASSIC PATTERN IN ALL OF THE THREE ISAIAHS

Let's revisit, in quick summary fashion, how the three Isaiahs each follow the prophetic development I have discussed thus far in the book. I encourage you to read the texts and, as I outlined in chapter 1 (page 13), use red, yellow, and green to highlight the patterns of order, disorder, and reorder.

ORDER (RED HIGHLIGHT)
"Holy, holy, holy!" (Isaiah 6:3)

- Assumes an eternal economy of "logical" and "deserved" reward and punishment. Holiness is defined as an absolute "purity" that cannot tolerate any "impurity."

- Presumes and even needs both a punishing and a rewarding God.

- The prophet's style is to threaten, accuse, judge, and promise retribution.

- Virtue and faithfulness are rewarded.

- *It is all about getting what you deserve, instead of getting who God is!*

HOLY DISORDER (YELLOW HIGHLIGHT)
"Now I am putting you in the fire like silver, I will test you in the fire of distress.... Never will I yield my glory to another." (Isaiah 48:10–11)

- The present is not working. People are still sinful and suffering.

- The world is not really changing.

- The prophets have doubts about what they thought was certain.

- Enemies are not always punished. Good is not always rewarded.

- God shows himself differently from how he's first imagined: more forgiving and merciful, it seems. One is either delighted or furious! Sometimes the prophet has a positive epiphany that changes his sense of God from anger toward compassion and lamentation (Isaiah 6).

- People experience exceptions to what they thought was the rule.

- It seems to be that those who have suffered and shed tears are those who move beyond this logic and find compassion in God.

REORDER (GREEN HIGHLIGHT)
"Open the gates! Let the upright nation come in. She, the faithful one whose mind is steadfast, who keeps the peace, because she trusts in you." (Isaiah 26:2–3, JB)

- A new economy of grace shows itself after observing how God operates.

- God "punishes" us by rewarding us even more!

- All forgiveness upsets the balance, our assumed economy of grace, our neat explanations.

- The only proper prayer is praise (for finally getting the point) and lamentation (for all who are missing the point). There is no judgment of anybody.

Again and again, after listing all their sins, Yahweh shouts almost in these words: *I could give up on you, but I will love you even more—and even more generously and undeservedly!* Some form of this is said at least a dozen times in Jeremiah, Isaiah, and Ezekiel. With that evolving realization of God's love, we plop into the new and everlasting covenant that is confirmed by the two other major prophets, Jeremiah and Ezekiel. The evangelists and Paul take this up in the rightly named New Testament (*testament* meaning "covenant") when they speak of "the new covenant in my blood which will be poured out for you" (Luke 22:20). The emphasis, I firmly believe, is on *my* blood—God's. In other words, on the pronoun and not on the noun! Sacrificial religion is over. Salvation (infinite love) is all God's work, and we must stop trying to renegotiate the terms to make ourselves more deserving. We never will be.

Isaiah is proclaiming a new illogical logic of unconditional love, and only those who make this leap can henceforth understand the nature of the divine bargain and our lives within it. "Very well," God says, "I will astound these people whose hearts are far from me with wonder upon wonder. The wisdom of your sages shall decay, the intelligence of your intelligent men will vanish" (29:14). God is finally allowed, as it were, to be infinite and gratuitous like the universe, and we are allowed to be the struggling and failing humans that we always are.

Now let's see how the other major prophet, Ezekiel, makes the same argument in a different way. He will emphasize personal responsibility like no prophet yet, while moving the doctrine of pure grace forward at the same time. His balancing act is quite an accomplishment.

CHAPTER 9

Ezekiel: Redemption and the Grace of God

The book of Ezekiel will never be a bestseller or a popular read, but it is essential to the whole canonical movement from a seemingly incoherent world—which the author's bizarre visions cleverly describe—to a universe filled with inner meaning and glory that we must know is shining through everything.

Ezekiel's prophecies are a good lesson in not throwing out the message because the messenger is a bit quirky. His eating of God's scroll of "lamentations, weeping, moanings" that became as "sweet as honey" (Ezekiel 2:10, 3:3); his extended "dry bones" metaphor for the whole house of Israel (chapter 37); his allegorical history of Israel as a beloved who nevertheless played the prostitute (chapter 16); his strange visions of intersecting wheels with eyes (1:15–21, 10:6–17); his vision of a traveling temple throughout the text—all make him a show not to be missed. One wonders, though, what his audience would have thought of such spectacles. He begins his book with disorder, not order, and one could honestly make a case for Ezekiel being on an early psychedelic experiment. By the end, though, he surely moves us toward a cosmic reorder, if we are willing to trust him.

Following the classic prophetic pattern, Ezekiel first emphasizes that God is angry at the people for their abominations and faithlessness, with the resultant punishment and retribution that will follow (chapters 4–12). In one of his first prophetic acts, he is instructed by God to lie on his left side for 390 days in public view, "bearing the weight" of Israel's sins; he then turns on his right side for another 40 days for the kingdom of Judah (4:4–6). So unworthy are the people that Yahweh actually leaves the temple in a huff at the end of chapter 10—completely unthinkable for the Jews of that time. (It makes me wonder what we Catholics would say if someone staged Jesus walking out of Saint Peter's in Rome. Probably we would imagine, *It's so pretty. Michelangelo everywhere! It's the biggest church in the world!*)

Ezekiel is a rare combination of priest and prophet. On one level, he emphasizes a rather complete distinction between sacred and profane, as priests are often wont to do. This may be because his prophecies took place entirely during the exile in Babylon (597–538 B.C.), when Israel was trying to hold on to its identity in a foreign land. It was an environment much like America's culture wars today, where social and religious boundaries beg to be neither worshipped nor thrown out. Ezekiel is still a practicing Jew, for sure. He holds on to his orthodoxy during the exile, but he does it in a most untraditional way, making startling breakthroughs like prevenient grace (Ezekiel 16:53–63) and individual responsibility (chapter 18), while still addressing Israel as "a set of rebels" against the law (12:1–9).

I almost find it remarkable that Ezekiel's text is even included in the Hebrew scriptures. It certainly shows the spiritual maturity, courage, and inspiration of the Jewish faith. I know of no other organized religion that is so willing to include accounts of its own faults and its critics and heretics in its sacred scriptures. We Catholics usually burned ours at the stake, while many Protestants just tuned them out and condemned them to hell. There had to be punishment, either in this world or the next, or our moral logic is lost! Ezekiel, though, manages to critique the law while showing obedience to it at the same time. One wonders how it worked out for him. (There is no account of how Ezekiel's life ended. He suddenly disappears from the scene around 570 B.C.)

The condemnations and anger toward Israel continue through most of Ezekiel's prophecies. Then, just when you think you cannot take any more lurid descriptions of the people's depravity, the scene utterly and for no apparent reason changes. In chapter 16, he suddenly says (speaking for Yahweh), "I will forgive all that they have done" (63). Like Jeremiah, he breaks the link we all suffer from: the notion that love must be earned, that we can create worthiness. Yet this infinite character can only be realized in doses.

All grace is prevenient grace—the kind that makes you desire or want grace to begin with! Grace is not what we deserve by doing the right things, but rather a gift freely given by the Creator in the very act of creation, even if we do not yet believe in its source. Knowing the source somehow just makes it easier to keep saying *Thank you.* As such, grace is, strangely, a punishment for the ego, which always wants to believe in payments and punishments, a concept we unfortunately got from religion itself. As Daniel Ladinsky renders Hafiz, "The sun never says to the earth, 'You owe me!' "[1]

Unlike the postcapitalist people that we are, Ezekiel even goes on to apply this notion of grace to the real-world economy. In chapters 13, 17, and 18, he condemns the practice of taking interest on loans (usury), calling it deeply sinful and untrue to the covenant. (Usury lasted as a mortal sin for the first thousand years of Christianity, but try telling that to your bank today, or to almost any Christian.)

Grace is one of those realities that is everywhere once you stop weighing, counting, and deserving. God's freedom to act freely is already highly visible in nature, in the movements of animals, the turning of seasons, and the profligacy of plants, once we stop to enjoy them. Such grace follows no logic, explanation, or even human decency. (Malodorous, ugly people are still beloveds to God!) Such freely given love is an ego humiliation that nevertheless leaves us ecstatic with new freedom, if we can only allow it. And it *is* an allowing.

Ezekiel affirms this unique and rarely understood notion of grace. Midway through the book, God speaks: "I am going to renew my covenant with you; and you will learn that I am Yahweh, and so remember and be covered with shame, and in your confusion be reduced to silence, when I have pardoned you for all that you have done" (Ezekiel 16:62–63).

Here, the people did not even ask for or recognize they might need forgiveness. When I first read this verse as a young friar, I was overcome by shock. *Why has no one even pointed out this break in our reward-punishment logic to me?* Ezekiel and Jeremiah were coming to the same conclusion around the same time, in the middle of the exile. Just when you think they would have been looking for reasons for such punishment, they broke out of its logic altogether. That's the refining power of suffering, I should think. "I will treat you as respect for my own name requires, and not as your own conduct deserves" (Ezekiel 20:44). God's only measure is Godself. We can never forget that.

In Ezekiel, Yahweh always acts and never reacts, as we humans tend to do. This is divine revelation at its fullest and freest! Restorative justice—the divine freedom to do good at all costs—is quite simply God being consistently true to God-self. It's a total end run around retributive justice, which Ezekiel portrays as being beneath God's dignity.

This theme of themes—God filling in all the gaps created by our ignorance, low self-esteem, and fear—reaches an apotheosis, in my judgment, in chapter 36. Here Ezekiel, at great length, completely *disqualifies* Israel as a partner by listing all their many adulteries. But immediately after stating Israel's total unworthiness, their constant and selfish prostitution of the ways of covenant, Ezekiel says that Yahweh completely requalifies the same relationship from Yahweh's side. It is a total disqualification and a total requalification at the same time, but both are God's doing:

> I will take you from the nations, and gather you from all the countries, and bring you into your own land. I will sprinkle clean water upon you, and you shall be clear from all your uncleanness, and from all your idols I will cleanse you. A new heart I will give you, and a new spirit I will put within you. . . . Then you shall live in the land that I gave to your ancestors; and you shall be my people, and I will be your God. (Ezekiel 36:22–38)

No reciprocity is any longer expected or demanded. God can't waste God's time anymore. It is all God's work and gift from beginning to end, if we are honest with ourselves. This is the promise of how God will work within history, and exactly why many of us firmly believe in "the universal restoration that God announced long ago through his holy prophets" (Acts 3:21, NRSV). That promise is then restated in mystics from Origen of Alexandria, to Gregory of Nyssa, to Julian of Norwich.

God works by the same pattern within the individual soul: forgiving and rewarding each of us "seventy times seven," in Jesus's words (Matthew 18:22). As the Israelites first realized after the Exodus, Yahweh is "a God of tenderness and compassion, slow to anger, rich in kindness and faithfulness and even "keeping steadfast love and forgiving faults and transgressions for the thousandth generation" (Exodus 34:6–7). Grace, like trauma, functions on an intergenerational scale. This is why so many of the mystics and prophets describe the body of Christ as being permanently crucified and permanently resurrected—first in the collective, and moving from there to individuals, both good and evil, until it eventually all melds back into the whole. I have worked with families whose love energy can be traced back to one holy grandparent. What if we all were to make that love energy our personal vocation? That would be a much better motivation for being good. Just as trauma is intergenerational, so also is healing.

As Ezekiel learned, and as I hope we can now see, God is saving history itself, and we are all caught up in this cosmic sweep. The prophetic tradition tries to make us see this by breaking all bonds and debts and shame about our past unfaithfulness. Trauma is held in the body, remember, and even in the whole body of Christ. We all suffer from one another's badness and enjoy one another's goodness. It is prophets and mystics who know that.

In chapter 34, Ezekiel emphasizes this pattern of divine action by comparing God to a good and healing shepherd:

> As shepherds seek out their flocks when they are among their scattered sheep, so I will seek out my sheep. I will rescue them from all the places to which they have been scattered on a day of clouds and thick darkness. I will bring them into their own land; and I will feed them on the mounts of Israel, by watercourses, and in all the inhabited parts of the land. . . . I will feed them with justice. (Ezekiel 34:12–16, NRSV)

We see that passage repeated in John:

> The gatekeeper opens the gate for [the shepherd] and the sheep hear his voice. He calls his own sheep by name and leads them out. When he has brought out all his own he goes ahead of them, and the sheep follow him because they know his voice. (John 10:2–4)

This Good Shepherd is promised at the very end of the exile, when the Israelites are hungry for tenderness and good pasture. They yearn not for a judge, but for a caring presence who can lead them out of danger—and it is given to them. *I myself will pasture my sheep*, says Ezekiel. *I myself will show them where to rest. I shall look for the lost one, bring back the stray, bandage the wounded, and make the weak strong* (Ezekiel 34:11–24, my paraphrase). What an astounding image of an almighty God! Later, Jesus uses this exact passage to describe himself.

In chapter 37, Ezekiel gives us the wonderful vision of the valley of dry bones to depict how such restoration might happen. "Yahweh . . . set me down in the middle of a valley, a valley full of bones," Ezekiel explains. "He made me walk up and down among them . . . the whole length of the valley. They were quite dried up. He said to me, 'Son of the Human, can you imagine it?'" (37:1–3) as if to say, *This is beyond human hope or imagination.* "These bones are the whole house of Israel," God later explains. "They say, 'Our bones are dried up, our hope has gone; we are as good as dead'" (37:11–12). Remember, the holding power of evil is in the collective! Just so, he instructs Ezekiel to do the "prophesying" over the bones of the whole nation. It is a good argument for the need for social justice and not just individual justice:

> Prophesy over these bones, make them live.
> Thus says the Lord God to these bones: I will cause
>   breath to enter you, and you shall live.
> (37:4–5)

Read the full text. It is like a Disney movie, with Ezekiel acting as the sorcerer's apprentice. It's almost as if God is allowing the prophet to take some credit for the miracle, even though God is clearly the primary mover in the partnership.

Here we have unearned restoration and renewal given by God to the exiles for the taking: "And you shall know that I am the Lord, when I open your graves, and bring you up from your graves, O my people. I will put my spirit within you, and you shall live, and I will place you on your own soil" (37:13–14). And this is still the case. Our job, too, is to breathe together with God upon the dry bones that are always present throughout our world and make them live, just as God has breathed on ours. (Mine now for over eighty years!)

IT'S ALL ABOUT EATING THE SCROLL

Last evening I watched a PBS special on the astounding mission of the James Webb telescope, which launched into space in 2021. What we once thought to be unreachable stars are now, through the telescope's lens, showing themselves to be unimaginable galaxies, thousands in every new moment's snapshot, which then reveals even more. The telescope was designed with "344 single-point failures"—each real possibilities for this object being hurled into space—and yet none of them have happened three years later! The machine is still out there, taking in the beauty of billions of light years and billions of galaxies.

I floated to bed in awe and humility at the building of this wondrous instrument. The only appropriate response to anything so seemingly infinite in skill and perfection is amazement, not understanding. God still lets us breathe together with him to produce seeming miracles.

I've wondered if such expansiveness was what Ezekiel intuited in his inaugural vision of wheels that "went forward four ways" (Ezekiel 1:17), moving "where the spirit urged them" (1:20). "I looked, and prostrated myself," the prophet says (1:28). Then he is given the scroll of "lamentations, weeping, moanings" (2:10), which he eats and finds as "sweet as honey" (3:3). Soon he is lifted up by the spirit and hears a tumultuous shout: "Blessed be the glory of Yahweh in his dwelling place" (3:12).

I read "eating the scroll" as a poetic way of describing "taking it all in": both the beauty of this awesome, moving creation and the joys and desolations of our tiny lives within it. *What is this divine and useless largesse all about?* one must ask. *What does it say about the nature of the Creator? What is the purpose here, and why did God take so long to show us the full body of God?* I suspect cosmology might now serve where philosophy and theology first tried. Ezekiel seemed to intuit what I feel when looking at the images from the Webb telescope.

The deep patterns and trajectory of creation become clearer and simpler over time, especially if you are listening through what many of us call contemplation or prayer. Think of prayer as an honest and continuous inner dialogue of the soul with the indwelling presence in all things. As the resurrected Christ breathed on his disciples and commanded them to receive the Holy Spirit (John 20:22), it is our very own breath—and God's, too—that we breathe on the dry bones of this world. The wheels are still moving, and their rims are covered with "eyes all the way round" (Ezekiel 1:18) as God grants gifts of seeing to human engineering, care, and curiosity. By the end of the Bible, these eyes have become "*all the way round* as well as inside" (Revelation 4:8). The outer world reveals the inner majesty, and the inner world displays the outer mystery, or what we might call full incarnation!

In an earlier chapter, we spoke of Carl Jung's use of alchemy as an effective metaphor for spiritual transformation. One of Jung's patterns is called *solutio:* the loss of one substance by becoming another (which, interestingly enough, became our word *solution*). Another is *conjunctio,* the combining of what seems like two until they become one. This might help us to understand this metaphor of *eating our words and fully digesting them.* The divine word *conjoins* with us, just as it later does in the womb of Mary (Luke 1:38a).

Jeremiah uses the same image of eating words and fully digesting them: "When your words came, I devoured them: your word was my delight" (Jeremiah 15:16). And it reappears at the very end of the Bible, when John eats the scroll that is bitter in the stomach, but in the speaking again "as sweet as honey" (Revelation 10:9–10). A new *solutio,* or solution, is offered to the speaker and the sincere listener, in this act of holding both the sour and the sweet together: hard truth and caring love, as I read it. In fact, we are being taught that *only love can handle the great truths.* All others misuse the appearance of truth for their own purposes—if their own thirst for power has not previously been definitively revealed and defeated by God and life. I think this is the most radical and substantial meaning of religious conversion.

For this book to have any transformative effect, it will be necessary to fully eat, absorb, and digest our experiences of organizing anger and disorganizing sadness, and then reorganize those deeply felt responses into praise and gratitude. Such transformation is always sweet in the mouth. This is the impact of God, and of God's prophetic speech. A major dose of reality is always good medicine, yet sour in the stomach, because we realize we are now responsible for what we have come to know. But the conjunction and the solution will always show itself as sweetness, because it is deep truth. Darn it! Universal responsibility would have been a so much better lesson than the almost completely universal damnation, which our present reading of the rules implies and predicts. For Ezekiel, the only reliable order is summed up in his final verse: "Yahweh is there" (48:35, JB).

I would hope Ezekiel might be a helpful teacher in our age of so many "wheels" and "eyes" moving in all directions. He is perhaps a prophet for the postmodern world we all now live in, where social media make us from childhood both the beneficiary and the victim of a thousand opinions. If he did not lose his mind and heart amid so much chaos, we don't have to, either.

Ezekiel is forever telling us, "Prophesy to the breath. . . . Come from the four winds, breath; breathe on these dry bones, and let them live!" (Ezekiel 37:9). Our love matters in this universe. Dry bones can still be remade with living flesh. It is God's very job description, I think. And now ours, too.

CHAPTER 10

It All Comes Down to Love

The early English Franciscan brother William of Ockham (1287–1347) had an overriding principle that is still taught in philosophy classes, and is somewhat humorously called "Occam's razor" (using the Latin spelling of his name). As he put it, "The answer that demands the fewest assumptions is likely the correct one." If his students wanted to discover the truth of something, he encouraged them to "shave" away as many assumptions, beliefs, or complicating explanations as possible. Great truth might well be mysterious, Ockham believed, but it is never complex. *The better answer is almost always the simpler one* was his conclusion.

What I have tried to say in this book is that prophets are those who simplify all questions of justice, reward, and punishment by a simple appeal to divine love. God's infinite, self-giving care is the only needed assumption, cause, factor, or possible variable in the drama of creation. All else must be "shaved" away as creating needless and useless complexity—which only confuses the soul and the mind.

This is the nature of mature, mystical religion—simple and clear. We shave away as many religious assumptions and judgments as possible and re-ground religion on one lone assumption—a divine love that can only be experienced and not proved by rational logic. The prophets claim to have had such divine experience and tell us that we can and must, too. This is their one absolute foundation and their radical center on which the entire rest of their message is built, and it makes them unlike any other kind of teacher. Anything that gets in the way of this divine and absolute love must be shaved away. This is the purpose of the sacred criticism practiced by Amos, Jeremiah, and the other prophets we have visited in this book.

How might we extend their work and legacy in our day? Unless we allow and encourage such people who are with us now, and in a mode quite different from our preference for angry rebels or prophets of doom, we will continue to create insular in-groups who are blind to their own shadow side—which is always and forever an inability to love the other. As we saw with many of their stories, the Israelites liked nothing better than to ignore the prophets and continue on their own sometimes corrupt and self-serving ways. The pattern is perennial. And we are exactly the same.

BECOMING CONSCIOUS

It's common for us to think of evil as an interruption of an otherwise smooth functioning order, usually caused by someone else. But evil and death are part of the deal—mixed in with all life, part of the common domain, shadowing all our best efforts and intentions. Death itself is an intrinsic part of existence. Idealists often cannot or will not see this, but prophets are not idealists. They are truth-tellers and utter realists.

We need to stop being surprised or shocked by reality and recognize that evil flourishes best when it is denied. Evil relies on being considered rational, necessary, and expedient by otherwise good people. Witness the ravages of communism and Nazism, when everyday people could not see how their shadow side, in completely different ways, was causing them to demonize and kill millions of their fellow humans. You can't see what your group can't see. But once you "out the demon" (the real hidden problem) in any group or on any issue, it loses much of its potency. Thus it should be no surprise when we identify evil with darkness—a state in which we cannot see—and goodness as a form of light, in which even our own darkness is illuminated.

This leaves us with a world of contradictions, if we look at it honestly. You can attack your chosen enemy and appear saintly or heroic, all while holding on to the same us-versus-them assumptions that got us into trouble to begin with. Love, however, is willing to accept and forgive a tragic sense of life. It does not allow a desire for the perfect to become the enemy and obstacle to simple goodness.

The nontragic sense of life gives easy and quick comfort, and it might "obliterate the angles of the crucifix," as Virginia Woolf says in her novel *The Waves*.[1] In the end, though, it does not really help, because it does not speak truthfully to the soul, as the prophets insist on doing. It is the opposite of contemplative thinking; such classic dualistic thinking relies on a inner and deeper light that they already possess. I am grateful we have learned to distinguish positive criticism from negative. I hope it has been clear in the stories of the prophets that growth and change are essential for them and for all of us. Process and growth are the only ways to make sense of inspiration, of our human biography, and of the very ordinary path by which we realize God.

It is wise, then, not to waste too much time looking for miraculous leaps forward in your own development, or waiting for the perfectly stated criticism that has no sting at all. Your ego loves that kind of thing, and its carping keeps many people from their best selves. Sometimes, if not always, the message we need comes in less-than-perfect packages. Across my many years in the Franciscans, as a pastor at the New Jerusalem Community, and as an employer at the Center for Action and Contemplation, I could create a long list of people who could not face their "personal prophets" and grow from their observations, even when wildly obvious to others. Most people, ourselves included, are very defensive in the presence of criticism. Both the shadow self and the ego self depend on denial and disguise, and are all well practiced at it.

GOD'S LOVE IS THE STANDARD

If Yahweh, the God of Israel, is as moody, inconsistent, petulant, and wrathful as many of us believe, and as much of the Bible seems to depict, then the whole universe is in major trouble. One could make the case that religion, along with being the best thing in the world for people who are inclined toward love, has also been the worst thing in the world for those who are still nursing grudges, wounds, resentments, and

rather complete denial of what it does not want to see, as we witness in so much American political speech today.

Paul was playing the prophet in Ephesians, when he said:

> Avoid the futile works of darkness by exposing
>   them.
> We are ashamed even to speak of our works of
>   darkness,
> But anything exposed to the light will be
>   illuminated,
> And anything illuminated turns into light itself.
>   (Ephesians 5:12–14)

We still need, and have, those who expose the works of darkness and speak uncomfortable truths to us with courage and a proper humility—the kind that leads to weeping, not anger, blaming, and shaming. They are not to be confused with the notion of saints, although the two roles often overlap in a single person. In the Catholic world, sanctity has been confused with moral perfection, but even that confuses the situation. I have met too many saintly people in a confessional context whose holiness is the result of years of struggle with their darkness and their ego, which they could never completely overcome. In fact, such folks are the quite obvious norm! Our job, like that of the prophets, is to guide their struggle toward love, not to deliver them altogether from struggle.

To be "children of light"—people in whom the gospel shines brightly—is different from being morally perfect or never failing. Any focus on perfection was an utterly false and illusory goal that made Christianity into a cult of innocence, whose adherents are so often full of blame and denial that they allow their fault to be projected onto others, unable to see similar failings in themselves.

When Jesus said we are "the light of the world" (Matthew 5:14), he said we must extend this light to "everyone in the house" (5:15) in the form of our own "good works" (5:16), not just exposing others' bad works. But light does what light does. It clarifies, helps us see fully, and gives us the insight, freedom, and courage to perceive ourselves rightly. Divine light does not inflate us with the pride of "I know," but illuminates those around us with the gratitude of "I am, too"— a kind of joining "everyone in the house." Both light and love reveal not our separate superiority, but rather our radical sameness. That quality is, in fact, the way you can tell divine light from human glaring.

Christianity is not a purity cult that we use to prove we are superior beings, although it has certainly seemed like that during its long history. Up to now, this has made far too many Christians into unconscious hypocrites, or what Jesus calls "actors." And I do mean unconscious; scapegoating is almost entirely an unconscious mechanism. The only way out of this mindset is quite simply to become "conscious," which in all world religions has to do with deep and existential self-knowledge that is almost always painfully gained. Socrates just called it "knowing thyself." Prophets help us to do just that— mercilessly toward their own ego and group.

See Matthew 23:13–29, where Jesus names the scribes' and Pharisees' hypocrisies, calling out their blindness and foolishness on issues of legalism, insincerity, cursing, "straining out gnats and swallowing camels" (verse 24), externalized morality, keeping up appearances, and killing those they pretend to follow, each stated in a most subtle way. He is not being mean

here, or rude, or even unfair. He is just encouraging them toward what Alcoholics Anonymous co-founder Bill Wilson calls "a fearless moral inventory."

We all have to admit we are prone to the same failings we see in others—and prone to deny them as well. This seems to be perennially difficult for us. "One after the other, the apostles say, 'Surely not I?'"(Mark 14:19) when Jesus announces that one of them will betray him. Without undergoing a fearless moral inventory, accompanied by some divine light and love of self and the other, you just cannot see your failings or hypocrisy. Creating scapegoats is the capital sin of capital sins, so much so that it required Jesus to become the cosmic scapegoat, exposing and resolving this dangerous and universal human illusion.

The death of Jesus, the crucified perfect person, stands as the Christian symbol of *the* scapegoating, which has always dominated human history. By placing this tragedy at the center of faith, we can join Jesus in saying, "Father, forgive them; they do not know what they are doing" (Luke 23:34). We will surely start with anger and disgust as we wake up to the universality of our fear and moral duplicity, but then we must let ourselves be moved toward a sadness and solidarity with the victims, if we can. Anger hardens, while sadness saves. The last veil to fall is when you see your own negative projections—not only your participation in the collective but also the hurts you've transmitted to others and yourself—and just want to weep. This is the universal solidarity and sympathy that I believe characterizes mystical and prophetic Christianity.

Unless we learn to see the "sacred criticism" of prophets as first of all, a gift given *out of love,* the very word *critic* or *criticism* will continue to have a negative connotation. It will be used to defeat the light in other people instead of revealing the

unforgiveness. They just assume God is that way, too, and it affects the world in tragic ways, as we have seen.

We must see the patterns of growth that are woven throughout the Bible and allow them to work on us, or we have a dangerous God who is mostly undoing the universe and making it unsafe, ungraceful, episodic, and unhappy for just about everybody. The Bible both demands that we grow up and allows our notions of God to grow up right along with it. Still not sure which comes first! We saw that growth in Jeremiah and Ezekiel, in the way God gives the people a new covenant of love. In the prophetic texts, God, like the prophets themselves, evolves from anger and fear to tears to love, and on to a deepening relationship based in trust and truth, not threat and fear.

Mature religion and good prophets make sure that this growth happens. They liberate us to be like God, who is love (1 John 4:8), and reveal that *God is not like us,* which is the purified message of almost every prophet.

We humans do not see things as they are; we see things as *we* are, and we have an unfortunate tendency to create God in our own image. Prophets are the ones who have allowed the radical decentering of their own selves, with their small preferences and priorities, in favor of another center that has shown itself as love—and even better, shown itself to be *in love with them.* They hope that every group would adopt the same decentered view of reality. But this is only possible if and when another radical center has shown itself to them: an absolute goodness and mercy that will always seem too good to be true! It is always, even for prophets, an epiphany that calls forth their own "Holy, holy, holy! . . . Heaven and earth are full of your glory!"(Isaiah 6:3).

Who of us knows much about love in the early years of our maturing? Who of us knows anything about truth when we just start to get educated in history, science, philosophy, or any other important topic? The ego cannot be presumed to read reality correctly at all. That is why most religions emphasize some kind of foundational conversion, transformation, enlightenment, new thought, rebirth, or different mind that all of us need to adopt. Like the prophets, we also must grow and change and move from dualistic anger to empathetic tears—and we must recognize that God has done the same.

In the New Testament, Jesus is shown weeping at least three times himself: once for the collective, "Jerusalem"; once for an individual, his dear friend Lazarus; and once perhaps for himself in the garden of Gethsemane (Luke 22:44). Did any religion ever offer its adherents a weeping God in all of history? Sorrow and pity do not seem to be included in the original divine job description.

Starting with the prophets and reaching its apex with Jesus, there is a clear message that humans cannot be the standard. In the place of our self-created morals and mythologies, Paul invites us to be imitators of God (Ephesians 5:1)—in Latin, *imitatio Dei*. And we are given some descriptions of what that might look like:

> If you, evil as you are, know how to give your children good things, how much more your Father in heaven. (Matthew 7:11)

> Be compassionate as your Father is compassionate. Do not judge and you will not be judged . . . grant pardon and you will be granted pardon. Give and there will be gifts for you. (Luke 6:36–38, JB)

I wonder if one reason why we have so effectively wrecked and misinterpreted Jesus is that we needed to prove he was the

Son of God or the Messiah or a miracle worker before we let him speak as a prophet. As artists have done in paintings over the centuries, we made Jesus conform sequentially to Jerusalem, Rome, Greece, Europe, and America, placing him in native costumes and reaffirming whatever worldview happens to resonate with us.

Once we took away the prophetic Jesus's counterintuitive message and his countercultural critique, he became the *personal possession* of every nation's biases, shadows, and preoccupations—hardly worthy of being Lord of the entire universe. Jesus ended up as an outsider in the eyes of Judaism, a theologian to educated Greeks, a competing warrior for Rome, a conquistador for the New World, a proper evangelical preacher for right-wingers everywhere, a white capitalist ally for the good old USA, a "best friend" for the therapeutic class, a harmless and optional teacher for many liberals, and the founder of a strange cult of innocence ("I am not a sinner") that almost no one can really live up to. Anything but a universal Christ for all of us broken sinners. And now people are leaving, no longer willing to drink this old wine.

The prophets—and Jesus—are the ones who have the courage to make God's way of loving action the source, the goal, the criterion, and the standard for all human morality and behavior. The questions for all of us should eventually be *What is God doing?* and *How does God act?* Asking such questions is a revolutionary mindset that demands some degree of inner experience of prayer and some contemplation of the natural world over time. These are the characteristics of a full spiritual life. And they are what makes prophets mistrusted and dangerous to any culture and religion in which the standards are invariably law, power, money, and personal advantage.

It was the prophets who started the move from religion to

spirituality that is becoming the norm in the West today. *Away with all easy formulas!* seems to be our reigning belief system, and I really see why. Often it is true and even good to reject formulaic belonging, and believing might just be the most salient form of disorder for our time. And we must admit that much of "old-time religion" has been replaced not by mere nihilism but also by a deep set of legitimate values that people sincerely live. I am meeting younger folk with such values everywhere, and I am hesitant to criticize them.

Of course, religion and spirituality do not need to be seen as opposites at all. But we are going to have to go through a serious replacement of "old wineskins"—the New Testament metaphor for the containers that hold religion—if we are going to let the world know we are sincere about reform and self-critique. "New wine demands new wineskins," says Jesus in Mark 2:22. But the "church on Sunday, Bible study on Wednesday, and not much else" model just cannot hold very much good or new wine. And in fact it does not, as we can see by the statistics of significant decline in religious affiliation.

A deeper and much-needed form of practice can no longer be confused with mere mandated attending and belonging. The liberating words of Jesus still ring in our ears: "The wind [or spirit] blows where it will . . . and that is how it is with all who are born of the Spirit" (John 3:8).

THE OBSTACLES TO LOVE

Only God knows if an opinion or person is genuine and true. Or, as Jesus puts it so well, "You can only tell if one is a true prophet by their fruits" (Matthew 7:16). In all honesty, that's kind of baffling! You can only see those fruits (and value) after the prophet has acted or spoken—yet we rarely seem to agree on those fruits. One group's freedom fighter may be another group's oppressor. One group's prophet is another group's deceiver. One group will see fruit, and another will see poison in the same event. Only authentic God people will recognize the true prophets from the false. "And who are they?" we naturally ask. This easily becomes another strong argument for not taking your judgments too seriously until you have studied and heard from other wise and loving people—including those who disagree with you.

Some might ask: *How is it that you believe human love is drawn from God, while human hatred is projected onto God? Isn't that just wishful thinking?* I don't suppose I can offer any foolproof argument, except for my general observations of human behavior. People who are already negative, cynical, or mistrustful tend to dislike religion and spirituality, even if they go along with them for familial or cultural reasons. People will gather reasons why any God talk is terrible, even when they are only half-right. People have hurt them, no doubt, but "God"—or their idea of God—has probably not. When people come to me with such complaints, it invariably turns out that I don't believe in the God they say doesn't exist, either. I usually feel a sincere sadness that they need to carry such a death wish for any kind of divine presence.

Already well-loved and loving people tend not to react against religion or spirituality. If they do jump in, they both improve it and use it to improve others, but you almost get the impression that neither do they need it! I think this explains for me that most problematic line at the beginning of Jesus's parabolic discourse: "Anyone who *has* [love] will be given even more and he will have more than enough, and anyone who does not *have* [love] will lose what little he has" (Matthew 13:12, emphasis mine). Here, Jesus makes a clear distinction between those who understand the point of his parables and those who can't. In short, lovers can and haters can't. (He'd surely better mean love, or he would sound more like a venture capitalist than a transformative teacher!)

If we project either our wrath or our moral capitalism onto God, the first thing to be destroyed is religion itself. That which was supposed to liberate now corrupts and diminishes. We become motivated by well-disguised self-interest and a lot of "againstness" instead of proceeding by way of trust or any real love. This seems to happen most commonly among the religions of "counting" and "measuring": Judaism, Christianity, and Islam in their most certain and dualistic forms (not so much in Indigenous peoples' religions, ancient Hinduism, or Taoism).

Please remember that certainty—not doubt—is the opposite of faith. The insistence on certainty reveals a need for control, not a need for love or understanding. Historians agree that much violence in human history has been religiously based, the predictable collision of two absolutely certain or dogmatic worldviews. Those views can be relied on to give us certitudes about our superiority, our judgments, and our actions, and they are also our most reliable justifications for scapegoating others. In light of such thinking, punishment becomes a moral mandate. If we are the loved ones and the "best," then the ever-present other has to be punished or eliminated. These are the obstacles to love that must be shaved away in all of us.

RECOVERING FAITHFUL CRITICS

We tend not to think of Jesus as a prophet because, as I have suggested throughout the book, we haven't understood or appreciated the prophet's unique job description in Israel: a "licensed," internal, faithful critic of one's own people and leaders. The prophets were radical traditionalists whose conservatism ironically made them into tearful and empathetic "progressives" by contemporary standards. They loved and honored Jewish customs, liturgy, and tradition, yet criticized the same mercilessly when they allowed people to ignore the poor and the oppressed. Recall the prophet taking this unusual stance in Isaiah 1:11–17 (see page 68). Or consider Jeremiah:

> Put no trust in delusive words like these: This is the sanctuary of Yahweh, the sanctuary of Yahweh, the sanctuary of Yahweh! . . . But if you do amend your behavior and your actions, if you treat each other fairly, if you do not exploit the stranger, the orphan and the widow (if you do not shed innocent blood in this place) . . . then here in this place I will stay with you. (Jeremiah 7:4, 6–8)

This is followed by a passage that Jesus quotes directly when he attacks corrupt practices within the temple: "Do you take this Temple that bears my name for a robbers' den? I, at any rate, am not blind" (Jeremiah 7:11, quoted in all three Synoptics: Mark 11:17, Matthew 21:13, Luke 19:46). But Jeremiah makes many similar critiques elsewhere:

> Monstrous, horrible things
> are happening in the land:
> The prophets prophesy falsely,
> the priests teach whatever they please.
> And my people love it! (Jeremiah 5:30–31, JB)

> "Peace! Peace!" they say,
> but there is no peace.

They should be ashamed of their abominable deeds.
But not they! . . .
They have forgotten how to blush.
Place yourselves on the ways of long . . . ago,
inquire about the ancient paths, which was the
      good way?
Take it and you will find rest. (Jeremiah 6:14–16, JB)

When we read the prophets, we Americans cannot tell if they are conservative Republicans or radical, liberal Democrats. They appear to jump back and forth, sometimes cautioning a return to tradition, other times urging radical departures. We seldom see such truth-telling prophets, mainly because there is no one to offer much internal and intelligent critique of their own side. No one expects that there could be such a thing. And yet we have been lied to and fooled so many times by uncritical leaders and governments that we are now in a major cultural crisis of truth. Maybe it is not even possible for us to believe that anyone ever speaks truth?

My hope and desire in writing this book is that we can recover the universal need for the role of prophet and prophetess in any group seeking moral authority, while also seeking to create and validate lovers and not just critics. We must learn to educate for the role of sacred criticism inside of secular groups—including nonprofits—as well as all religious organizations, so that prophets can move all our institutions toward health. The great irony is that many totally secular organizations protect whistleblowers in their ranks much more than most churches, synagogues, and mosques do. It is written into many of their constitutions and policies.

We probably need to come up with better titles for prophets than *devil's advocate*—or even *prophet,* for that matter. We need a name that connotes a person who is wholesome, educated on the issues, both insider and outsider, the loyal opposition who knows how to be loving and respectful toward all sides. We need someone who is on the loving but critical edge of any developing in-group, a truth-seeker who has dealt with his or her own wounds. Wounded healers are what we need. Wounded wounders, not at all.

Maybe such a new way of seeing would help us reclaim Jesus as the prophet of Christianity and thus reclaim Christianity itself as an *ecclesia reformata sed semper reformanda:* a religion that speaks of reformation not in the past tense, as something that happened once or twice in Europe, but something that is always reforming itself—by necessity. The fruit of that reformation should be that the world says, as Tertullian did, "See how they love one another!" (Apologies 39). And that love must include critiquing one another's failings with respect and restraint.

A DEEPER GOSPEL OF UNCONDITIONAL LOVE

My final conviction is that we cannot dismantle the violence we see in the world if we allow threats and promises to be the overarching frame of Christianity, or any religious or secular creed. This dualism—the idea of an infinite God being caught up in a naïve reward-punishment worldview—must be undone by the deeper gospel of unconditional love and respect, or nothing will ever change. We will not, we cannot, understand or absorb the compelling message of the prophets so long as we allow fear, threat, and self-interest to dominate the story.

Can a pious pro-lifer ever admit that war, capital punishment, and social justice are also pro-life issues? Can the political left ever recognize its therapeutic bias, its individualism, its rejection of transcendence, its lack of support for the common good? Our small, myopic agendas have nullified the triumphant work of grace for too long. So I would like to end with a parable that shows how it looks when our new and everlasting covenant is reordered entirely in love.

In my first years of preaching in the early 1970s, I often told a little story that was called "The Angel with the Torch and the Pail." Just last week, an old friend reminded me that it had changed his life and his religion. He had never forgotten it, and he wondered if I still spoke of it in recent decades. I had not. So here it is again—short, unembellished, and directly to my point:

> An angel was walking down the streets of the world carrying a torch in one hand and a pail of water in the other. A woman asked the angel, "What are you doing with that torch and pail?"
>
> The angel said, "With the torch I am burning down the mansions of heaven, and with the pail I am putting out the fires of hell. This is the only way we will ever know who really loves God."

Something must break us out of the reward-punishment frame. It is too small and too self-serving. It makes the God of the ever-evolving and expanding universe seem equally small and petty, and it has already shown itself to create far too many small, petty, largely competitive, and happily vengeful humans. Yet, in spite of it all, the universe remains one giant self-revelation of the fabulous nature of God, not a small stage where one slice of the human species can show itself to be a winner or a loser.

Somehow, the loving people I have met all across the world seem to know that if it is love at all, it has to be love for everybody. As soon as you even begin to parcel it out, you are not in the great field of love.

> The prophets want us to love God above all else,
> And be loved by God above all other partners.
> Which will, and must, lead to a universal love.
> The kind that sets out to rescue those we'd much
>   rather condemn.
> That is the prophets' hard-won conclusion,
> Their tear-filled victory.
> Is there any other kind of winning?

A GOOD SUMMARY

In chapter 10, I wrote that the Jewish prophets inaugurate a critically different notion of religion, with two distinct but complementary roles of priest and prophet. The priests, like Aaron, create and maintain the religious container. The prophets, like Moses and Miriam, make the container worth preserving and enjoying. While the two roles might seem oppositional at first, they actually transcend any dualism if you understand them in their mature forms. The prophets do not oppose the priests, but they are not co-dependent on them either, another example of their nonviolent genius. The priests must not suppress the prophets, or their own real message is lost.

Below, I have gathered together some of the qualities that indicate a true prophet. This list extends beyond the prophets of the Old Testament to the qualities of prophets in any age and any tradition. I have explored many of them throughout this book, but I offer the list at the end to bring some synthesis to my analysis, and to help the reader crystallize what even to me has often seemed complex—because it is so utterly new to the ordinary psyche, I believe.

Analysis without synthesis is often useless, unhelpful, or far too critical.

Synthesis without analysis is often false comfort and even untrue.

The prophets showed they were masters at both.

THE WAY OF THE PROPHET

Prophets embrace religion as a way of creating communities of solidarity with justice and suffering.

They look for where the suffering is and go there, just as Jesus did.

They speak of solidarity with one God, which also implies union with all else.

They are essentially mystical and unitive, not argumentative.

The goal they proclaim is not to prove oneself worthy, innocent, or pure.

The prophet learns to be *for* and *with,* and not against.

They are *for* those who are suffering or excluded.

They have perfected the art of self-criticism, and they make it their priority.

They include the opposites and thus transcend them.

Salvation, to them, is the unitive consciousness in this world, not the anticipation of later rewards or fear of future punishments.

They are centered not on sin but on growth, change, and life.

They know that the best teachers are reality itself and creation.

They live well with paradox and diversity in their mature stages.

They do not reject the way of the priest—they have just moved beyond it alone.

They are not based in fear of God or self.

They are always drawn to higher levels of motivation.

Salvation is, first of all, experienced now, as are rewards and punishments.

They start with judgment but end with the divine pity.

They call forth tears more than anger.

The tears of everything.

And those tears are more tears of gratitude and joy than tears of sadness for what might have been.

The Prophets of Israel

B.C.	Prophetic Speakers	Prophetic Narratives
1200	MOSES (both a prophetic speaker and a prophetic writer)	Miriam
1100	Deborah (primitive account in Judges)	
	Samuel (anoints David)	
1000	Nathan (confronts David)	
875	Elijah/Elias (action and contemplation symbol)	
	Elisha (successor of Elijah, role can be taught to others)	
	Prophetic Writers	
760	Amos (social justice)	
750	Hosea (steadfast love)	
730–700	I ISAIAH, chapters 1–39 (against false religion and temple)	
	Micah ("karma" of good and evil)	
630	Zephaniah (humility and the little poor ones will triumph)	
615	Nahum (gives warnings, and calls to justice and faith)	
600	Habakkuk (both the oppressor and the oppressed are evil)	
	JEREMIAH (the reluctant prophet)	Book of Lamentations
587–536	EZEKIEL (the eccentric prophet)	
exile in Babylon	II ISAIAH, chapters 40–55 (Jesus's favorite)	
	Obadiah (example of two steps backward, vengeful "prophet")	
	Haggai (rebuilding after devastation)	
520	I Zechariah, chapters 1–8 (reconstruction theme)	
500	III ISAIAH, chapters 56–66 (sets a trajectory toward universalism)	
	Joel (judgment and restoration)	Jonah (universalism)
450	Malachi (moralisms)	
		Job
300	II Zechariah, chapters 9–14 (scattered fragments collected)	
	Baruch (hopes of those now in dispersion)	
165	Anna (prophetess living in the temple, integration figure)	DANIEL (apocalyptic)
5	John the Baptizer	
4	Jesus of Nazareth	

All dates are approximate

SEVEN THEMES OF AN ALTERNATIVE ORTHODOXY

The following seven themes from among my many teachings provide an honest statement about the underlying foundations of what I teach.

1. Scripture (as validated by experience) and experience (as validated by tradition) are good scales for one's spiritual worldview (*methodology*).

2. If God is Trinity and Jesus is the face of God, then it is a benevolent universe. God is not someone to be afraid of, but is the ground of being and on our side (*foundation*).

3. For those who see deeply there is only one reality. By reason of the Incarnation, there is no truthful distinction between sacred and profane (*frame*).

4. Everything belongs. No one needs to be punished, scapegoated, or excluded. We cannot directly fight or separate ourselves from evil or untruth. Darkness becomes apparent when exposed to the light (*ecumenical*).

5. The "separate self" is the major problem, not the shadow self, which only takes deeper forms of disguise (*transformation*).

6. The path of descent is the path of transformation. Darkness, failure, relapse, death, and woundedness are our primary teachers, rather than ideas or doctrines (*process*).

7. Nonduality is the highest level of consciousness. Divine union, not private perfection, is the goal of all religion (*goal*).

ACKNOWLEDGMENTS

"How do I thank thee? Let me count the ways."

For my theological and philosophical education, it all goes to the Franciscan Friars, over many years, for whom I am most grateful. You taught me how to think both inside and outside of the biblical and Franciscan tradition.

For exposure to generations of probing students, I thank both the New Jerusalem Community in Cincinnati, fifty years of teaching on the road from 1973 to 2023, and fifteen years in the Living School of the Center for Action and Contemplation in Albuquerque, New Mexico.

For making me love the prophets, I especially thank Abraham Joshua Heschel and Walter Brueggemann for their brilliant and courageous scholarship.

For any verbal access and coherence of thought in this book, I thank Sheryl Fullerton for her deep caring for both the message and for me, and Derek Reed of Convergent/Penguin Random House, who exhibited all the skills a really good editor should be known for, along with our own CAC publications manager Mark Longhurst. They all deserve major applause for staying with this octogenarian mind so kindly and so patiently. Thanks also to everyone at Convergent who gave their time and care to the publishing of this book.

And to borrow from Elizabeth Barrett Browning, I thank thee with the breath, smiles, tears, of all my life; and, if God choose, I shall but thank thee better after both fans and critics have their say.

NOTES

EPIGRAPH

1. Rosemerry Wahtola Trommer, "For When People Ask," in *All the Honey: Poems* (n.p.: Samara Press, 2023), 39.

INTRODUCTION

1. Judaism often identifies Sarah, Miriam, Deborah, Hannah, Abigail, Huldah, and Esther as prophets.
2. Richard Rohr, *The Wisdom Pattern: Order, Disorder, Reorder* (Cincinnati: Franciscan Media, 2020), 3–22.
3. Richard Rohr, *Falling Upward: A Spirituality for the Two Halves of Life,* 1st ed. (San Francisco: Jossey-Bass, 2011).
4. Ken Wilber, *Integral Meditation: Mindfulness as a Path to Grow Up, Wake Up, and Show Up in Your Life* (Boulder, Colo.: Shambhala Publications, 2016).
5. René Girard, *Violence and the Sacred* (Baltimore: Johns Hopkins University Press, 1977).
6. Richard Rohr, *The Divine Dance: The Trinity and Your Transformation* (New Kensington, Penn.: Whitaker House, 2016).
7. Brené Brown, *Daring Greatly: How the Courage to Be Vulnerable Transforms the Way We Live, Love, Parent, and Lead* (New York: Avery, 2015).
8. As quoted in Joseph Campbell, *The Inner Reaches of Outer Space: Metaphor as Myth and as Religion* (Novato, Calif.: New World Library, 2002), xxiii.

1. THE TEARS OF THINGS

1. Shared in a 2008 essay broadcast on BBC Radio 3 as part of the Greek and Latin Voices series.
2. Steven Charleston, *We Survived the End of the World: Lessons from Native America on Apocalypse and Hope* (Minneapolis: Broadleaf Books, 2023), 9.
3. Ken Wilber, *A Brief History of Everything* (Boston: Shambhala, 2000), 56.

3. A CRITICAL MASS: THE SECRET OF THE REMNANT

1. The Holy See, Pontifical Messages 1958, First Radio message, October 29, 1958, www.vatican.va/content/john-xxiii/en/messages/pont_messages /1958.index.html.

4. WELCOMING HOLY DISORDER: HOW THE PROPHETS CARRY US THROUGH

1. Richard Rohr, *Falling Upward: A Spirituality for the Two Halves of Life*, revised and updated (San Francisco: Jossey-Bass, 2024).
2. Richard Rohr, *The Naked Now: Learning to See as the Mystics See* (New York: Crossroad, 2009).
3. Richard Rohr, *Eager to Love: The Alternative Way of Francis of Assisi* (Cincinnati: Franciscan Media, 2014).
4. Charles Eisenstein, *Sacred Economics: Money, Gift & Society in the Age of Transition*, rev. ed. (Berkeley, Calif.: North Atlantic Books, 2021).

5. JEREMIAH: THE PATTERNS THAT CARRY US ACROSS

1. Matthew 21:13, Mark 11:17, Luke 19:46.
2. Richard Rohr, *The Universal Christ: How a Forgotten Reality Can Change Everything We See, Hope For, and Believe* (New York: Convergent Books, 2019), 16.
3. Richard Rohr, *Hell, No!*, audio CD (Albuquerque, N.M.: Center for Action and Contemplation, 2014).
4. Richard Rohr, *Falling Upward: A Spirituality for the Two Halves of Life*, 1st ed. (San Francisco: Jossey-Bass, 2011).

6. UNFINISHED PROPHETS: ELIJAH, JONAH, AND JOHN THE BAPTIZER

1. Quoted in Edward W. Desmond, "Interview with Mother Teresa: A Pencil in the Hand of God," *Time*, December 4, 1989, https://time.com/archive /6703981/interview-with-mother-teresa-a-pencil-in-the-hand-of-god/.
2. Richard Rohr, *Adam's Return: The Five Promises of Male Initiation* (New York: Crossroad, 2004).
3. Richard Rohr, *Job and the Mystery of Suffering: Spiritual Reflections* (New York: Crossroad, 1996).
4. The Qu'ran, trans. Talal Itani, 4:163.

7. THE ALCHEMY OF TEARS: HOW WE LEARN UNIVERSAL SYMPATHY AND GRACE

1. Gerald G. May, *Will and Spirit: A Contemplative Psychology* (San Francisco: Harper & Row, 1987).
2. Carl G. Jung, ed., and M.-L. von Franz, Joseph L. Henderson, Jolande Jacobi, Aniela Jaffé, *Man and His Symbols* (1964; repr. New York: Bantam Books, 2023).

3. Dorothy Day, *On Pilgrimage* (Grand Rapids, Mich.: Eerdmans, 1999), 84.

4. Richard Rohr, *The Naked Now: Learning to See as the Mystics See* (New York: Crossroad, 2009).

5. Carl G. Jung, *The Collected Works of C. G. Jung,* vol. 12: *Psychology and Alchemy* (Princeton, N.J.: Princeton University Press, 1953).

8. THE THREE ISAIAHS: THE HEART OF PROPHECY

1. William Blake, "Auguries of Innocence," in James Fenton, ed., *William Blake: Poems* (London: Faber and Faber, 2010), 90.

2. Abraham Joshua Heschel, *The Prophets* (New York: Perennial, 2001), 12.

9. EZEKIEL: REDEMPTION AND THE GRACE OF GOD

1. Daniel Ladinsky, *The Gift: Poems by Hafiz the Great Sufi Master* (New York: Penguin Compass, 1999), 34.

10. IT ALL COMES DOWN TO LOVE

1. Virginia Woolf, *The Waves* (London: Hogarth Press, 1931, 1960), 133.

ABOUT THE AUTHOR

RICHARD ROHR is a globally recognized Franciscan friar and ecumenical teacher whose work bears witness to the deep wisdom of Christian mysticism. He is the founder of the Center for Action and Contemplation in Albuquerque, New Mexico, an educational nonprofit dedicated to introducing seekers to the contemplative Christian path of transformation. Rohr is the author of numerous books, including the *New York Times* bestseller *The Universal Christ*. His work has been featured on Oprah's *Super Soul Sunday* and *On Being with Krista Tippett*, and in *The New Yorker* and *Harper's* magazine.

THE CENTER FOR ACTION AND CONTEMPLATION

Transforming Ourselves, Each Other, and the World

Richard Rohr founded the Center for Action and Contemplation (CAC) to support his vision of transformed people working together for a more loving, just, and connected world.

Located in Albuquerque, New Mexico, the CAC serves as a gateway to spiritual development by offering seekers an introduction to the wisdom and practices of the Christian contemplative tradition. Our programs and resources are designed to provide spiritual guidance in support of inner and outer transformation. When we apply this wisdom in practical ways, we discover healing and are empowered to become instruments for love and positive change.

By carrying forward Richard's founding vision, we believe the CAC can become a catalyzing force for change of consciousness inside Christianity and each of our communities. This work invites each of us to play a part—a whole body, a whole community, a whole movement of people grounded in shared vision, values, and an experiential knowing of God's presence in our life showing up in the world together.

Learn more at cac.org and help co-create a world where everything belongs.

Wherever you are on your spiritual journey—that's where God is.